Dedication

This book is lovingly dedicated to my wife and the mother of our six children:

Sandra Joy Corley Moore,
The First Lady of Prayer,

. . . and the one who has time and again proven herself to be *Prayer Force One* in my life.

"Better to beat the drum than be the leader of the band."

Ed Moore

Table of Contents

Part I - The Mission of Prayer Force One

Part II - The Message of Prayer Force One

Part III - Appendixes

Ed Moore

Forward

The book you have before you is probably unlike anything you've ever read before. Part personal story, part history book, part revival manual, part study guide; it is a call to spiritual action in order to save our nation. Only God knows what will become of the dreams that are presented in this book. In humility, and on the wings of many prayers, Sandy and I offer this book and this movement to our LORD and to our country. The disposition of these dreams, we leave to Him.

The book is written in three parts. The first part tells the story of the birth and growth of *Prayer Force One* to date.

The second part seeks to recapture and champion the Christian heritage of the United States. This section is presented in seven lessons complete with quizzes for personal and group Bible study. This section is also graphically organized so as to provide a ready reference resource for those who are in a position to promote and defend the spiritual heritage of America.

The third part consists of several appendices. In this section, we have outlined how to become active at the local level by starting a Prayer Force One *Prayer Wing* in your home or church. We have also included a clear presentation of the gospel of Jesus Christ in the hope that it will be a help to those who would seek salvation.

I wish to thank my wife, Sandy and my family for sharing both husband and father, not only in the writing of this book, but also for the heavy traveling schedule that lies yet before us. I also wish to thank the many wonderful people of my church, who have unselfishly shared their pastor with the larger calling. Finally, a big thanks to all who have unselfishly worked, given and prayed for the birth of *Prayer Force One*. These are too numerous to mention, but not forgotten.

To you, the reader, I send this book forth with the prayer that it will encourage many to become involved in the great effort of saving the spiritual foundations of our country. May we and our nation obtain Heaven's mercy and favor through sincere and humble prayer. God please bless America once again!

Ed Moore
Newalla, Oklahoma
January 12, 2007

Once to every man and nation,
Comes the moment to decide,
In the strife of truth with falsehood,
For the good, or evil side. . .

Then it is the brave man chooses,
While the coward stands aside,
Till the multitude make virtue,
Of the faith they had denied.

Excerpt from a poem by:
James Russell Lowell, 1849

Part I

The Mission of
Prayer Force One

"If my people, which are called by my name, shall humble themselves, and pray, and seek my face, and turn from their wicked ways; then will I hear from heaven, and will forgive their sin, and will heal their land."

II Chronicles 7:14

9

THE WHITE HOUSE

WASHINGTON

June 1, 1981

Dear Senator Moore:

Together we have won a great victory for the country with the bipartisan votes on the budget in the House and the Senate. Your support at home was a key to that victory and I want to thank you for it.

I was pleased that you were able to attend the briefing here in Washington on the Economic Recovery Program. The Vice President enjoyed meeting with you, and I'm disappointed that I did not have a chance to visit with you also when you were at the White House. I hope you'll understand that I was doing a little "recovering" of my own at the time.

It is great to be getting back to a full schedule and it is particularly gratifying to be working with talented and articulate state and local leaders as we forge a new spirit of federalism for this Nation. I am counting on your continued active support as we move on to the next crucial component of the economic package, tax reductions.

Best personal regards.

Sincerely,

Ronald Reagan

The Honorable Edward B. Moore
2720 Southwest 39th
Oklahoma, Oklahoma 73119

Shown here is a letter I received from President Reagan in which he makes a rare and historic reference to the March 30, assassination attempt on his life. Notice the date is just eight weeks after the shooting.

10

Chapter One
"The President Has Just Been Shot!"

"President Reagan has just been shot!" These were the words that greeted me as I walked onto the floor of the Oklahoma State Senate on March 30, 1981.

"You wish." I replied in good humor to my senate colleague. We often sparred in jest inasmuch as we were complete opposites where political philosophy was concerned. I was considered a Christian conservative while he labeled himself, a social liberal. Just the same, we got along very well. He was actually a very nice guy.

I expected a good comeback in equally good humor. Instead he replied, *"No, I'm serious, they've just announced it on the radio."*

I looked at his face and immediately knew that he was quite earnest. We both rushed past the senate podium, across the reception area and into the private senate lounge where other senators were already gathering around the television set. We, along with millions of other Americans, watched as the now familiar video footage of the assassination attempt was first being shown. The gravity of the situation dawned on each one of us as we stood in silence. The voice of the television announcer was all that could be heard.

Then, at that moment, something wonderful happened, something that was repeated all across America. Someone simply said, *"Let's pray."* Instinctively, the senators present reached out and joined hands. Republicans joined hands with democrats. Conservatives joined hands with liberals. Urban senators joined hands with their rural counterparts. We were men and women, both black and white. In

11

that moment, nothing divided us, we were all just Americans united in prayer for our nation and for our president. In that moment, the men and women in that room represented more than just a slogan which said, *"United We Stand."* In that prayer, we were all sincerely saying, *"In God We Trust;"* and, I think God was pleased. I believe God heard and answered our prayers that day, as well as the prayers of millions of others across America.

As I walked back up the steps to my senate office on the fifth floor of the capitol, my mind raced back to the first time I had actually seen Ronald Reagan in person. It had been in 1976, during the American Bicentennial. At the time, Reagan was challenging President Gerald Ford for the Republican nomination. I had arrived in Tampa Bay, Florida for a speaking engagement when I discovered that Reagan was scheduled to appear at a local mall. The influence of that event would later serve to redirect the entire course of my life.

Not long after Reagan lost the G.O.P. nomination, I wrote to him from Sydney, Australia where my wife and I had just arrived as church planters with Baptist International Missions, out of Chattanooga, Tennessee. While there, I wrote and encouraged Reagan to run again in 1980 and said that we would be back in the states by then and that we would do all we could to help get him elected.

Although my letter was no doubt like thousands of others, Reagan wrote me back. Maybe it was because it was from Australia. Maybe he answered all such letters, I don't know. Regardless, he wrote me back and I have always treasured that letter. Little did I know at the time that when 1980 rolled around, I would be on the same ballot in a political race of my own. We would both be elected on the same night. He to the presidency, while I became the youngest man ever elected to the Oklahoma State Senate. I actually out-polled Reagan within my district, winning a seat in the senate that had never been held by a member of my particular party. I have often jokingly said that Reagan rode my coattails. The opposite, of course, was true. But, let me get back to the day of the assassination attempt.

When I walked into my office that day, my wife, Sandy, was on the phone. She was calling to tell me that Reagan had been shot. Again, we prayed. We talked of how we had seen the Reagans only a few months before when we were part of the delegation that represented Oklahoma at the 1981 Presidential Inauguration.

   We had decided to drive to the inauguration so that we could take our three children with us. Off we went in our mini R.V., a 1977 Dodge Santana camper van. We arrived in Washington D.C. at about three in the morning and parked on Independence Avenue about half way between the Capitol Building and the Jefferson Memorial. Then, with a view of the Washington Monument glowing in the nighttime capitol sky, we crawled into our overhead bed and joined our children in welcome sleep, to await the inaugural sunrise.

   The next morning we awoke to all kinds of activity. The inauguration was to take place on the west steps of the capitol for the first time in history. We could easily see the inaugural stand from where we had parked. When it was nearly time for Ronald Reagan to take the oath of office, I joined my family on a grassy knoll not far from the bottom left of the capitol steps. Michael Reagan, the President's son, describes the scene better than I could ever do:

   "On the day of his inauguration as the fortieth President of the United States, Dad raised his right hand, placed his left hand upon the well-marked Bible of his late mother, and took the oath of office as prescribed by the Constitution. The Bible was open, and his hand rested on the words God spoke to King Solomon in II Chronicles 7:14:

   'If My people, which are called by My name, shall humble themselves, and pray, and seek my face, and turn from their wicked ways; then will I hear from heaven, and will forgive their sin, and will heal their land.'

   In the margin next to that verse, his mother Nelle had written, 'A most wonderful verse for the healing of the nations.' America was in need of healing on that wintry day in January, 1981. The nation badly needed to be healed - morally, spiritually, economically, and militarily."

   In The Words of Ronald Reagan, by Michael Reagan
   (Thomas Nelson Publishers, 2004, pp. 62-63)

It was at this point that something amazing happened in the sky overhead, Sandy and I witnessed it first hand. I again turn to Michael Reagan's book as he quotes from a *Time* magazine account:

"As he raised his head to look out at the crowd, a strange and wonderful thing happened. The dark cloudy sky over his head began to part slightly, within seconds there was a gaping hole in the dark overcast, and a brilliant, golden shaft of wintry sun burst through the clouds and bathed the inauguration stand and the watching crowd. As Reagan spoke, a slight breeze ruffled his hair and the warm golden light beamed down on him.

Later, a few minutes after he finished speaking, as if on cue from some master lighter backstage, the hole in the clouds shrank, the sky darkened, and Washington grew gray and cold once again."

(Quoted from, *In the Words of Ronald Reagan,* by Michael Reagan, Thomas Nelson Publishers, 2004)

Before continuing, I feel it necessary to describe something that Ronald Reagan had done earlier at the Republican National Convention in Detroit, Michigan on July 17, 1980. After delivering his acceptance speech for the Republican nomination for president, Reagan paused and then said:

"I'll confess that I've been a little afraid to suggest what I'm going to suggest, [pause]. . . what I'm going to say. But I'm more afraid not to. Can we begin our crusade joined together in a moment of silent prayer?"

[The audience then arose with heads bowed for a few moments, after which Ronald Reagan concluded:]

"God bless America!"

Soon after his inauguration, while speaking at the Conservative Political Action Conference in Washington D.C. on March 20, 1981 President Reagan said, and I quote: *"Evil is powerless if good men are unafraid."* Little did the President know that just ten days later, he would be used to prove how true those words were. Not even an assassin's bullet could bring down a president who had been unafraid to ask for prayer before a nationally televised audience.

When Ronald Reagan recovered from his gunshot wound he wrote in his diary *"Whatever happens now, I owe my life to God, and will try to serve him in every way I can."* His son, Michael Reagan, writes that his father told him shortly after the assassination attempt, *"I believe that God spared me for a purpose. I've made a decision to recommit the rest of my life, and the rest of my presidency to God."* (Ibid)

Several years later, Sandy and I finally had the privilege to meet President Ronald Reagan and to sit down with him in the Green Room of the White House. A White House photograph of that meeting hangs proudly in my office to this day. On that day, my wife and I were privileged to meet, first hand, the President who was spared in answer to our prayers and the prayers of millions of others.

Perhaps you remember where you were when Ronald Reagan was shot. Such events have a way of making lasting impressions on our memories. I can vividly remember exactly where I was as an eleven year old boy, when the word came that President John F. Kennedy had been assassinated. I had been on my way back to grade school from lunch in my hometown of Blackwell, Oklahoma, when my fifth grade teacher, Mrs. Stephenson, offered me a ride. No sooner had I closed the car door, when the ABC radio announcer broke in with the news that Kennedy had been shot. Some of my readers are old enough to remember exactly where they were at that moment too. My teacher simply said, *"We need to pray for our country."*

I can also remember exactly where I was when the Federal Building in downtown Oklahoma City was bombed. I remember hearing the blast, and feeling a puff of moving air across my face several miles from the site. I remember seeing the plume of dark, angry smoke rising in the distance. Years before, I had lived in the Athenian Building, at the very spot where the truck bomb was detonated. Like many others, my first instinct was to pray for those in harm's way. Later, Evangelist Billy Graham and President Bill Clinton came to our city to lead in a municipal prayer service for the families of those who had perished.

No doubt, almost every one of you can remember the events of 9/11, which were followed by an outpouring of national grief and many prayers. By that time, my oldest son was a fireman in the city of Moore, Oklahoma. Understandably, he told me that he could remember praying for the many New York City firemen as they rushed in to save the people in those towering infernos. Perhaps you can remember offering up prayers for those in New York City, in Washington D.C., and in the charred fields of Pennsylvania.

The point is this: *Why does it seem to take a national disaster to unite Americans in prayer?* Why must we wait until some horrible event jolts us into acknowledging our nation's need for God's help? Is it not possible to recognize today, right now, that our country cries out for us to kneel down in united prayer? The truth is that a national dilemma is upon us even now. The clear reality is that we are at the crossroads of either losing or reaffirming our national spiritual heritage. The choice that we make will determine whether we are to continue with the blessings of the LORD God, or condemn ourselves and our children to the curse of all nations that forget God.

It was no accident that Ronald Reagan selected II Chronicles 7:14 as the Bible verse upon which he would lay his hand on that wintry inaugural morning. The thing that we must remember is that the promise of II Chronicles 7:14 is just as true today as when it was written over 3,000 years ago. However, there is a contingency. We must remember that the promise begins with an *"if"*. God's promise begins with: *"If My people, which are called by My name, shall humble themselves and pray. . ."* National renewal must begin with national prayer. This is our part. This we can do. This we must do. This is the need of the hour.

It has now been some twenty-five years since Ronald Reagan first took the oath of office. Perhaps the greatest lesson and parting legacy of his life can be summed up in his own words when he said:

"I do not believe in a fate that will fall on us no matter what we do. I do believe in a fate that will fall on us if we do nothing."

(First Inaugural Address, January 20, 1981)

The book you now have in your hands is about *doing something*. More importantly, however, it is a book about doing something God's way. This is a book about saving a nation, about returning to the God of our fathers. This is a book about the power of prayer when we obey the admonitions of II Chronicles 7:14. This is not a book about President Ronald Reagan, Senator Ed Moore, or any other politician. It is a book about the American people, and whether or not we will return to our spiritual heritage and the faith of our fathers. Again, let me be very clear. This is not a book about political parties or political action. It is not about political candidates or political agendas. It is not even a book about getting involved in the American political process. This we should do because we are good Americans.

On the contrary, this is a book about calling America back to God. It is a book that seeks to challenge Americans to both call their nation to prayer, and then to pray for their nation. *Specifically, this book is a call for Americans to join together in a national prayer meeting to be held on the Sunday before the next Presidential election, and before every subsequent national election thereafter.* What could possibly be wrong with that? Or more correctly, should I not ask: *"What could be more right?"*

For this reason, we have named our book, *Prayer Force One: Across America.* We have done so because prayer *is* force one; because our prayers have greater force when we pray *as* one; and because we must martial our prayers into a force *of* one on behalf of our nation. We say, *"Across America"* because this is the message that we seek to deliver all across our land, and because we will only succeed if Americans everywhere, themselves embrace this great call.

Benjamin Franklin said, *"If a sparrow cannot fall to the ground without His (the Lord's) notice, is it probable that an empire can rise without His aid?"* I believe this; and it's just as true about the advent of our President and other leaders. This book will seek to explain what the Bible says concerning this great truth, and in what way we are encouraged to participate. Just as surely as a diverse group of Oklahoma State Senators could join hands and pray on that awful day in March of 1981, so too, we as Americans can and must join our hearts in prayer to God on behalf of our ailing nation.

Allow me to tell you how this vision was born, and then to ask you to join me on a spiritual and patriotic journey across America aboard *Prayer Force One.*

Prayer Force One, Spring 2006

"There be three things which go well,
yea, four are comely in going:
a lion which is strongest among beasts,
and turneth not away for any;
a greyhound;
an he goat also;
and a king,
against whom there is no rising up."

Proverbs 30:29-31

Chapter Two
"Call The Bus Prayer Force One."
The Story Behind The Birth Of Prayer Force One

"I've got to turn around." I said excitedly to my wife.

"Why?" She responded, wondering what in the world I was thinking.

"Did you see that greyhound bus in that empty field?" I asked.

"No," she replied, *"but I have a feeling that I haven't seen the last of it either."* It's funny how she knows these things. That little outing to the city turned out to be a turning point in our lives.

Sam Ray, of *The Texans*, an award-winning gospel group from Branson, Missouri was the one guilty of getting me interested in buses. When I say buses, I am referring to the commercial cross-country buses like the ones used by Greyhound and Continental Trailways. When I first met Sam, he and his wife, Brenda, and the group were singing their way from church to church across America using an old GMC motor coach to travel in. On their second visit to our church, their bus had developed a problem en-route, and he had only barely nursed the bus into our church parking lot.

The next day, I posed a question to Sam's feet, which extended out from under the bus. *"Sam,"* I asked, "*why do you travel around in this old bus instead of getting yourself a proper motor home?"*

Sam rolled out from under the bus, sat up and told me what he thought every educated American ought to know. *"Ed,"* he said, "*this may look like just some old bus to you, but these babies were engineered to go 24/7, seven days a week, twelve months a year, year after year, and to do it in safety and style. When all those glitzy new motor homes are sitting on the side of the road, this old bus will still be bending the highway. Sure you have to work on them sometimes.*

But, when it comes to serious cross-country road work, these babies are in a league of their own."

"Hey Sam," I replied apologetically, *"I didn't know."* I had just had my first lesson about buses and bus people. I never looked at another greyhound bus the same after that; and what is more, unbeknownst to me, I had just been bitten by the bus bug. This is a disease from which the afflicted party seldom, if ever, recovers. I understand that it is somewhat akin to the incurable affliction commonly known as *"Potomac Fever."* After that, I became interested in buses and prided myself on being able to identify the make and model of almost every commercial bus on the highway. This was my state of mind on that cold winter day in November of 2004.

My wife and I did turn around and after a little inquiry, found out that the bus belonged to a man who owned a septic tank company. He had only recently acquired the bus from Oklahoma Baptist University. *"That means she's been properly maintained."* I told Sandy, and then added, *"I like a bus with a spiritual pedigree too."*

"I'll trade you a houseboat and $2,000 in cash for the bus," I offered the man, *"but,"* I added, *"you'll have to install a septic tank on my property to boot."* He accepted the offer and we were both happy with the deal. After charging the batteries and thawing out the air lines, she started on the first crank. She purred like a big cat, and turned out to be as sound as a five dollar gold piece.

For those interested, the bus is a 1971 M.C.I. MC-7 Challenger with an 8V-71 Detroit diesel engine. It is what Greyhound referred to as their *Super-7 Scenicruiser* and later as the first of their *Americruisers.* I personally believe that she is the most beautiful and functional coach ever built. She entered service the same year as *Amtrak,* which was also the last year of Burlington's *California Zephyr* and Santa Fe's *Super Chief.* Ronald Reagan had used an MCI bus to launch his political career in both his 1966 and 1970 races for governor of California. Curiously enough, our coach was built at the same time as *Air Force One*, SAM 27000, which now resides at the Reagan Presidential Library in Simi Valley, California. But I'm getting away from my story.

In the weeks and winter months that followed, I became strangely conscious that a serious sense of spiritual destiny lay in store for us as it related to that bus. On more than one occasion, I told my wife, *"I don't know why God gave us that bus, but I know it's for a very special reason."* I didn't know what that reason was, but I did begin to pray and ask God to show me why He had given us the bus.

Someone once said, *"God works in mysterious ways, His wonders to perform."* To this day, it still amazes me at how God can insert *"tab A"* into *"slot B"* at just the right time. I know, of course, that there are theological terms to describe this, but the wonder is that it happens in all of our lives, whether we are aware of it or not. Perhaps God brings the right person across our path at just the right time. Perhaps God puts an idea into our head that just won't go away. Sometimes, a thing may lie dormant, deep within our unique individual makeup, while we are only vaguely aware of some slight sense of destiny. Whatever you wish to call it, that's the way I came to view that big, 40-foot bus in our driveway.

Then one day, all became crystal clear. The last of our six children, Tyler, had just started another year of baseball practice. On the way to practice, we had gone by the library where I had picked up a National Geographic DVD entitled, *Air Force One*. Since it was quite chilly on the day of that early spring practice, I climbed into the back of our van and slipped the DVD into the player. Sometime between the start of that program and the end of baseball practice, I heard the still, small voice of the Spirit of God whisper, *"I want you to name the bus Prayer Force One and call America back to Me."*

No, I did not hear an audible voice, but it was that same inner voice of the Spirit of God that had called me to Christ when I was sixteen years of age. It was that same quiet voice that later called me into the ministry. This phenomenon is not unique to me; I might add. It is the birthright of all of God's children. The Bible says, *"For as many as are led by the Spirit of God, they are the sons of God."* (Romans 8:14) Jesus said, *"My sheep hear My voice. . . and they follow me."* (John 10:27) One of the greatest Biblical illustrations of this is to be found in the story of Elijah.

"And He said, Go forth and stand upon the mount
before the LORD. And, behold, the LORD passed by,

> *and a great and strong wind rent the mountains, and*
> *brake in pieces the rocks before the LORD; but the*
> *LORD was not in the wind: and after the wind an*
> *earthquake; but the LORD was not in the earthquake:*
> *and after the earthquake, a fire; but the LORD was not*
> *in the fire: and after the fire a still small voice...And the*
> *LORD said unto him, Go...*"(I Kings 19:11-12,15a)

I believe that every Christian is led of the Spirit of God. Some listen better than others, but the voice of God is there just the same. Every true believer knows what I am talking about. On that day, I believe I heard the still small voice of God instructing me to prepare that bus for an odyssey across America. I was to join others in a much larger effort to call America back to God. II Chronicles 7:14 was to be our Biblical mandate. Those who were supposed to hear would listen. There was yet hope for America because there is hope in God. I was only too glad to get to be a part.

I have to say that I was immediately overcome by the immensity of the project. I walked excitedly up and down the ball field, contemplating the audacity of the idea. What if no one would believe me? Would this not be considered a great presumption on my part? I felt like Moses who basically said, *"LORD, who's going to listen to me?"* (Read Exodus 3:11 & 4:1 & 10, etc.)

I went back to the van and called my wife, Sandy, and told her of the vision. Having been raised as a missionary's daughter, she simply said, *"Well, praise the Lord."* That is just her way. She is as solid as a rock, and my lifelong encouragement and friend.

There would be much to do in order to call America to a national prayer meeting on the Sunday before the next Presidential election. The date was just over three years away. A book would have to be written in order to share the vision. We would have to convert the bus and prepare her for the road. Funds would have to be raised. People would need to be recruited. A web site would have to be built. There was so much to do and so little time in which to do it.

It was just at this point that we began to see some very peculiar blessings of God upon our efforts. Let me relate just one story by way of example. We decided that if we were going to call our bus

Prayer Force One, we at least ought to try and match the paint scheme used on the President's plane. It was Jacqueline Kennedy who had requested the famous industrial designer, Raymond Loewy to come up with the livery for the presidential jet. Loewy had become famous for his many beautiful designs, which included everything from Coca Cola's logo to the Pennsylvania Railroad's famed *Broadway Limited*. Strangely enough, it was also Loewy who had designed the paint scheme for Greyhound's first scenicruisers.

As I said, Sandy and I wanted to match the colors on Air Force One. To do this we took a trip to see our daughter, Randi, and husband, Jonathan, who were training for the ministry at California Baptist University, in Riverside, California. While there, we went to the Ronald Reagan Presidential Library, where Air Force One (SAM 27000) was being refurbished for permanent display. When we got there, we were surprised to find that the plane was actually being prepared for her new coat of paint. Unfortunately, we were also disappointed to find that we would not be allowed to get anywhere close to the plane. However, one of the security guards in sympathy with our project, winked as he quietly informed us that the company in charge of painting the jet had trucks parked in the public parking area. Sure enough, there they were, with the telephone number of the home office painted on the side of each truck. We called the firm in Georgia and told the owner of our plans and the need for a color match. After an initial hesitation, he suddenly did a one-eighty, stating that he had just ordered eighty gallons of paint for Air Force One. He said that if we didn't mind going back to Oklahoma via Las Vegas, Nevada, we could have ample quantities of all four colors of the actual paint used on Air Force One.

So now you have it: Prayer Force One is painted with the exact same paint as Air Force One. This may seem like a little thing to you, but for us, it was just one of many small miracles that God repeatedly used, and still uses to confirm His blessings on our endeavors.

Years before, while working my way through Hyles-Anderson Bible College in the Calumet region near Chicago, I worked at the famous Pullman-Standard railroad car company. This is the same company that pioneered and manufactured the magnificent Pullman sleeper cars and fine dining cars of the great age of rail travel. Using the knowledge that I had gained there, as well as my many years as a carpenter, we spent the next nine months converting the interior of the bus. I designed the floor plan in such a way that the bus would not only have private accommodations, but could be used as a traveling dining car and conference center as well. It was clear from the outset that we would need these beautiful yet practical accommodations as we went from state to state, making appearances at various governors mansions, and state capitols, in churches and bookstores, and in holding press conferences. In the front half of the bus, we placed a twenty-seat dining area complete with lighted Washington monuments to serve as lamps on each of the four dinettes. We placed the galley in the middle of the coach which was followed by our private quarters in the back. (See photos on pages 102 & 103)

We installed twin General Electric refrigerators, and decided to called them *Ronnie* and *Nancy* in honor of Reagan's G.E. days. Don't worry, we're bipartisan, we decided to call our generator *Truman* because we purchased it several miles from the Harry Truman Presidential Library in Independence, Missouri. The conversion was a beautiful success and immediately began to catch the attention of all who saw her.

However, it is important to point out that we could never have gotten so far on so little had it not been for the sacrifice and help of the many wonderful Christian people who unselfishly pitched in to make the dream come true. We are so thankful for Jeremy Simons, who did a magnificent job of painting the coach. I had had the privilege of leading Jeremy to the Lord in his living room only the year before. Jeremy had been with me when we first laid hands on the bus and claimed it for Christ. God soon began sending other people such as Paul Stephens, a brilliant computer technician, who volunteered to design our web site and then to head up our audio-visual department. These are only a few of the great people that God began to send our way in order to to prepare for the launch of Prayer Force One.

The President's plane, called SAM 27000, known as *Air Force One* and our MCI Challenger were both built and put into service at the same time in 1971-72. So also, both of them saw a rebirth of duty in 2005-06. SAM (Special Air Mission) 27000, which had flown seven presidents, was refurbished and given to the American people for permanent display at the Ronald Reagan Presidential Library. Our MCI, Super-7 Americruiser, which we call SHM 27000, (Special Heavenly Mission, pronounced "*Sam*") was refurbished to enter into service as *Prayer Force One*. If and when we ever acquire a new bus, we will call it SHM 28000, in keeping with the numbering of today's presidential jet.

When the conversion was finally completed, my oldest son, Corley, good-humoredly asked me. *"Dad, if the President's plane isn't technically called Air Force One until the President steps aboard, does the bus not become Prayer Force One until you step aboard?"*

He was kidding, of course, as he poked fun at my ego, and I took his ribbing in good stride. But you know, I really did begin to think about the role that each of us can play in the ministry of praying for our country. In spite of the many sentimental similarities and obvious differences between Air Force One and Prayer Force One, the one really great difference is that anyone can become a part of Prayer Force One. After all, God's call is to each and every believer, from the humblest, to the most influential.

As the ministry of Prayer Force One advances across America, I ask you to remember that prayers fly higher than any Presidential jet. They soar to the very throne of Almighty God. The ministry of Prayer Force One is necessary in order to encourage all Americans to join together in prayer for God's favor and blessings upon our country. America is not so far gone that God cannot save us, but He will only save us if we are willing to obey His voice and cry out with ours.

Allow me to close this chapter with an old familiar sentence which comes to my memory often. We all know it, for we typed it time and again during typing class in High School. We typed, *"Now is the time for all good men to come to the aid of their country!"* This has never been more true than it is today. Now *is* the time for all good men, women, teenagers and children, to come to the aid of their country. We believe that the greatest aid of all is that of getting on our knees before God, and praying for our nation. To this end, we sincerely ask for your prayers, and for your help. We hold the door open. Welcome aboard *Prayer Force One*.

"There was a little city, and few men within it; and there came a great king against it, and besieged it, and built great bulwarks against it. Now there was found in it a poor wise man, and he by his wisdom delivered the city."

Ecclesiastes 9:14-15

Chapter Three
A Shining City On a Hill

"Ye are the light of the world. A city that is set on a hill cannot be hid." (Matthew 5:14)

I would like to ask you to think of America as a single shining city on a hill. This is the way that John Winthrop saw it in 1630 from the windswept decks of a tiny, little ship called the *Arabella*. This was before there was a New York City, or a Boston, or Chicago, or St. Louis, or Dallas, or Denver, or Los Angeles. This was before there was a George Washington or a Thomas Jefferson, or an Abraham Lincoln, or a Theodore Roosevelt. This was long before there was a Declaration of Independence, or a United States Constitution, or a Bill of Rights. This was before there were steam locomotives or automobiles, or airplanes; before farms, and sawmills, and steel mills and manufacturing plants. For America, at least, it was almost before time.

Across the deck rails of the *Arabella* lay a vast wilderness, a brave new world, with the promise of a bright and glorious future. As John Winthrop peered out into the night he penned his vision for the new world in his diary. Then, just before going ashore, Winthrop shared his vision and this stern warning to his fellow pilgrims:

> *"We shall be as a city upon a hill. The eyes of all people shall be upon us, so that if we shall deal falsely with our God in this work which we have undertaken, and so cause Him to withdraw His present help from us, we shall be made a story and a byword through all the world."*

President Ronald Reagan also used the phrase *"A Shining City On A Hill"* as a beautiful metaphor for America. He referred to John

27

Winthrop and quoted his words on more than one occasion. In his Farewell Address to the nation, on January 11, 1989, President Reagan said:

> *"In the past few days when I've been at that window upstairs, (in the White House) I've thought a bit of the 'Shining City on a Hill.' The phrase comes from John Winthrop, who wrote it to describe the America he imagined. What he imagined was important, because he was an early pilgrim, an early freedom man. He journeyed here on what today we'd call a little wooden boat; and like other pilgrims, he was looking for a home that would be free. I've spoken of the shining city all my political life, but I don't know if I ever quite communicated what I saw when I said it. But in my mind it was a tall, proud city built on rocks stronger than oceans, windswept, God-blessed, and teaming with people of all kinds living in harmony and peace; a city with free ports that hummed with commerce and creativity. And, if there had to be walls, the walls had doors, and the doors were open to anyone with the will and the heart to get here. That's the way I saw it, and see it still."*

Then, as President Reagan continued, he asked:

> *"And how stands the city on this winter night?"*

I believe that every generation of Americans must answer this question from time to time. We have been handed a free and wonderful country. A windswept country, yes, but a country God-blessed too! But, like all free nations, we are not impervious to the perils that accompany freedom. Tonight, as I write, I sit aboard Prayer Force One. Outside my window it is cold and snowy. I too ask myself, *"How stands the city on this winter night?"* Outside, a great battle is raging. Tonight, there are two forces that seek to destroy the shining city on a hill. The first are the forces of external hate, jealous of America's freedom and America's destiny. These are forces of darkness which through acts of violent terror seek to burn the shining city to the ground. Americans need never fear such cowardly foes.

From within, however, we face a very different danger, a clear and ever present danger. John Winthrop, the same one who envisioned America as that *"Shining City on a Hill"*, also warned against our greatest enemy. He called it the act of *"dealing falsely with our God."* By this we understand him to mean the act of invoking the blessings of heaven, and then with ingratitude, forsaking Him, while taking credit for ourselves.

Today, within America, a battle is raging for the soul of our nation. On the one side there are those good people within the city that seek to keep faith with our God. These still acknowledge the providence of God in the history and affairs of our nation. This historic recognition is overwhelmingly evident as attested to by the words of our forefathers. (See lessons one and two in Part II)

On the other side however, the forces of immorality and godlessness strike at every vestige of public acknowledgment of God. These would remove *"Under God"* from our Pledge of Allegiance. They would take *"In God We Trust"* off the face of our currency. These would deny our state legislatures and even Congress itself the right to begin their sessions with public prayer. These same forces would deface our granite monuments by blotting out the chiseled acknowledgments of our fathers to Almighty God. Worse yet, these enemies do all of this in the name of the very liberties that their actions, left unchecked, will destroy. To these forces, nothing is sacred, and there is nothing they would not dishonor, including life itself. America must ever confront these destructive voices from within. Again, I quote Ronald Reagan. Listen to his warning.

"Without God, there is no virtue, because there is no prompting of the conscience. Without God, we're mired in the material, that flat world that tells us only what our senses perceive. Without God, there is a coarsening of the society. And without God, democracy will not and can not long endure. If we ever forget that we are one nation under God, then we will be a nation gone under."

(Republican National Convention
Dallas, Texas, August 23,1984)

As I have stated, when I heard the voice of the Spirit of God calling me to the ministry of Prayer Force One, I was immediately overwhelmed. To be honest, I had become somewhat cynical concerning America's future. In some ways I felt like saying, *"What's the use?"* But then again, my wife and I have six children, and as of this writing, nine grandchildren. How could we say no to the call of God? If decent, God-fearing Americans give up, who then will come to our country's defense? Edmond Burke, put it this way: *"All that is necessary for the triumph of evil, is for good men to do nothing."*

But, I faced a greater challenge yet. How could I ever hope to succeed? And, who would possibly help me? This fear was a formidable apparition. Then it dawned on me. A great prayer movement could itself only succeed if it moved forward on its knees. I therefore knelt in prayer and asked God for His wisdom.

I did not have long to wait. Several nights later, as I lay in bed in the wee hours of a sleepless night, an obscure and unfamiliar passage of scripture came to my mind. I could not remember it all, but the part that I did remember kept going over and over in my mind. It said, *"There was a little city . . . There was a little city. . ."* I could remember little else about the scripture except that Solomon had been the writer and that it had something to do with wisdom. I knew instinctively from experience, that the answer to my prayer lay in that passage. I arose from my bed, and slipping into my housecoat, I carried my Bible to my desk and turned the lamp on. When I finally found the location of the passage I also found the blueprint for Prayer Force One. Allow me to quote the scripture passage, and then give you the interpretation of what God revealed to me that night. As I do, I hope that you will see yourself in the story.

> *"This wisdom have I also seen under the sun, and it seemed great unto me: There was a little city, and few men within it; and there came a great king against it, and besieged it, and built great bulwarks against it. Now there was found in it a poor wise man, and he by his wisdom delivered the city; yet no man remembered that same poor man. Then said I, Wisdom is better than strength: nevertheless the poor man's wisdom is despised, and his words are not heard. The*

*words of wise men are heard in quiet more than the
cry of him that ruleth among fools. Wisdom is better
than weapons of war: but one sinner destroyeth much
good."*   (Ecclesiastes 9:13-18)

Now first, we must get a picture of the situation firmly in our
minds. Solomon, the wisest man who ever lived outside of Christ,
was telling us of an event that he had personally observed. There was
"a little city," and *"few men in it."* By this we are given to understand
that the city was both vulnerable and ill defended. The fact that it had
few men in it may be taken literally or as a metaphor to describe the
lack of those willing to defend her.

Whatever the case, we also see that a great dilemma faced the
city, for *"a great king"* had come and *"besieged it"* and *"built great
bulwarks against it."* By this we come to understand the great and
overwhelming odds that the city faced. No doubt the situation
appeared hopeless to the inhabitants. Soon, their beloved city would
be starved into submission and overcome by superior forces. Her
defenders would be slain by the edge of the sword. Her women would
be ravaged by the enemy, and her children carried off into slavery.

However, something happened that changed the entire outcome
of the battle. As it turned out, there happened to be a poor wise man
living within the city gates. By the words concerning his poverty,
and by other comments about him, we are given to understand that
this man was both ill-esteemed and considered totally inadequate to
offer any kind of hope. Nevertheless, we are told that he turned the
tide, and won the victory for the city.

The Power Of Prayer

Now, the question is this: how did this poor man do it? How did
he deliver the city? If we can answer this question, we will have the
answer to our own country's dilemma today. When we first look over
the story, it doesn't seem to tell us what this wisdom was . . . or does
it? It certainly doesn't give us any clue as to how the victory plan
worked, nor how he convinced the people to trust him. However, we
are told this: *"And he by his wisdom, delivered the city."* Now, if we
read this as simply, *"he by his wisdom"* we will miss the significant

secret that led to victory. But, if we read it as, "he by HIS wisdom" (meaning God's wisdom) we have our answer. You see, the wisdom was God's! The Bible says,

> *"For the LORD giveth wisdom: out of His mouth*
> *cometh knowledge and understanding. He layeth up*
> *sound wisdom for the righteous: he is a buckler to*
> *them that walk uprightly."*   (Proverbs 2:6-7)

Although we don't have the details of the plan that won the day, we do know that the winning wisdom came from God. But what did it consist of? I prayed about this for some time, and when the answer came, I was shocked at its simplicity. Do you know how he delivered the city? I believe that he told them to do exactly what II Chronicles 7:14 said to do! He told them to repent and to pray! After all, these are the very words that God gave to Solomon in a special vision by night. (See II Chronicles 7:12-14.) Whatever else this wisdom consisted of, rest assured that it first began with prayer. This is exactly what saved the children of Israel at the Red Sea. (Read Exodus 14:10) This is exactly what saved the Gentile city of Nineveh. (Read Jonah 3:5-10) I believe that this can also save America today.

The Power of One

But, let us get back to our story of the little city on a hill, for there is more to learn. Notice, that this great deliverance came by way of a single individual. Please don't misunderstand. We are all just single individuals. Because of this, the poor wise man in the story represents each and every one of us. He represents you. He represents me. Until we come to the place of recognizing our own accountability as part of the society in which we live, we will never understand how God responds to the consensus of a nation. After all, no society ever yet had a referendum on the ballot that said. *"Will we serve the Lord? Vote yes or no."* Yet, every day we cast a vote by our actions, and by our prayers. God himself keeps a tally of the vote.

It is for this reason that God can say, *"Blessed is the nation whose God is the LORD."* (Psalm 33:12) You see, God does take notice. And, just as surely as God can bless a nation, he can also curse and punish one. The Bible says, *"The wicked shall be turned into hell, and all the nations that forget God."* (Psalm 9:17) What concerns me is that this nation is on a fast track to forgetting God. This is what John Winthrop warned us about.

Remember too, that the wise man of Solomon's story also represents the hope that each of us brings to bear upon the plight of our nation. This one man made a difference. You can make a difference too. Sure, you are just one. So am I. Sometimes we don't feel like we can make a difference, or that we even count. But take heart, nobody is two! We must never underestimate the power of one when that one is aligned with God. The great Apostle Paul said, *"I can do all things through Christ which strengtheneth me."* (Philippians 4:13) Although one sinner can destroy much good, (which is how our story concludes) so too, one good man or woman can also turn the tide of battle.

Do you remember the story of Esther? The whole nation of Israel was to be destroyed when God raised up a young Jewish girl for the sole purpose of saving her people. Her Uncle, Mordecai, made an appeal to her sense of duty as well as to her sense of destiny when he asked, *"Who knoweth whether thou art come to the kingdom for such a time as this?"* (Esther 4:14)

I ask the same of each of you. Remember, that you could be the very one to tip the scale in the direction of victory. God puts great dividend upon the importance of the individual. Each one of us must do what we can if we are to make a difference. Someone has said,

> *"I am only one; but, I am one. I cannot do everything;*
> *but, I can do something. And what I can do, I ought to*
> *do; and by the grace of God, I will do!"*

The Multiplied Power of Two

The next bit of wisdom that can be gleaned from our story is that of the multiplied power of two. The Bible says, *"How should one chase a thousand, and two put ten thousand to flight, except their Rock had sold them, and the LORD had shut them up? "* (Deuteronomy 32:30) If you do the math, you'll find that two working together are ten times more powerful and effective than one man working by himself. The trouble is that God's people are divided while the enemy is uniting on every front. This has to be overcome. This must be corrected. Are we to believe that our sons and daughters from every geographical, ethnic, and religious background are expected to put on a uniform and unite in defense of our country, but that Christians cannot put aside their differences to unite in prayer for their nation? God forbid! Whatever wisdom the poor wise man used, we may rest assured that the citizens of the city united in the plan which brought the victory. So also we must unite in prayer.

When God is on our side, no one can prevail against us. This is exactly what Paul referred to when he said, *"If God be for us, who can be against us?"* (Romans 8:31) But God will only come to our aid if we do what He says. That is what II Chronicles 7:14 is all about.

The Stuff Of True Greatness

The last thing that I wish to point out about the story of the poor wise man who delivered the city is this. The Bible tells us, that for all of his efforts, no one remembered that same poor man, and that his wisdom was despised. This seems so sad. This seems terribly unjust. Yet, even here, there is wisdom to be found.

The truth here is that genuine greatness does what it does, despite the consequences; despite the fact that our efforts are often unrecognized and unappreciated. Leadership that achieves in spite of this reality is what true greatness is all about. The Bible says that God honors the man *"that sweareth to his own hurt and changeth not."* (Psalm 15:4) True greatness goes the distance regardless of the consequences and without the applause of men. One of Ronald Reagan's greatest and most oft repeated quotes echoes this principle of unselfish leadership. He said:

"There's no limit to what a man can do or where he can go if he doesn't mind who gets the credit."

Each one of us must remember this lesson as we spread the message of Prayer Force One. We can make a difference if we don't mind being ridiculed and abused, or even unrecognized. The truth is that it really doesn't matter. We are not here for vain glory or the applause of men, but to save our nation.

The Rest Of The Story

We began this chapter with the story of John Winthrop. Now, like Paul Harvey has so often said, permit me to tell you the rest of the story. Two days after stepping ashore in the New World, John's son, James, drowned in a river, the first of three of his children to die. With much of their supplies ruined by the voyage. John sent a letter back on the ship to his son in England, It read, *"Send food now!"* But it would be many months before the ship could cross the great Atlantic and then return from England. During the hard winter that followed, hundreds died. The whole company was tottering on the brink of starvation. Still, John Winthrop kept faith with God. Despite criticism, hunger, sorrow and despair, he held his surviving band together in prayer. In February, the last of their supplies ran out. As John Winthrop put his hand into the barrel to pull out their last cup of grain, someone cried out, *"Its here!"* At that very moment a ship arrived bringing a new supply of food to the colony. John Winthrop distributed the food and then proclaimed a day of thanksgiving. Over the next ten years, twenty thousand settlers poured into the Massachusetts Bay Colony in what was to become the cradle of liberty. The rest is history.

My fellow Americans, as I write these words aboard Prayer Force One, there is still hope for America. This is because that within the American soul, there has always resided an underlying faith in God. This is what our enemies have always failed to recognize. Even as our nation drifts from her spiritual moorings, there is yet hope. The enemy has come in like a flood. But, take heart, this is just when God has promised to show Himself strong. In Isaiah 59:19 the Bible says, *"When the enemy shall come in like a flood, the Spirit of the LORD shall lift up a standard against him."* This promise is unto all them that *"turn from transgression"* (verse 20). II Chronicles 7:14 gives us God's blueprint for national revival. The only real question remaining is this: Are we willing to get serious about meeting God's conditions. Are we really ready to fight the spiritual battles necessary to save the shining city on a hill? Perhaps the question I pose in the next chapter will help you to determine just how serious you really are!

Sandy and I at the door of Air Force One. (Sam 27000) We believe that every American should be as just as committed to the future of America as if they themselves were running for the office of President of the United States.

Chapter Four
"Will You Run For President?"

*"The whole land is made desolate, because no man
layeth it to heart."* (Jeremiah 12:11)

I want to ask each and every reader to consider a very important question. What would you say, if a group of civic, business and religious leaders were to come to you and sincerely ask you to run for President of the United States? Now I know that for most of my readers, this question must seem absurd. Just the same, I sincerely ask you to indulge the thought for the duration of this chapter. As you do, I believe that you will force yourself to look at your own patriotic duty and commitment from a new and revealing perspective.

Again, all things being equal, and provided you had the necessary credentials to be a serious candidate for the presidency, what would go through your mind? Suppose the group said that they thought you were just the right person, and that they would extend the necessary initial funding to get your candidacy off the ground. Suppose they asked you to think about it for a week before giving them an answer. Would you dismiss the idea outright or would you at least mull the idea over? How would such a decision effect your life, your family and your future?

The first thing that you would have to consider would be the loss of your personal privacy. In fact your whole life to the present would become an open book subject to public scrutiny and criticism. The press would look under every rock; comb through your private finances; second-guess every word you had ever uttered and every decision that you had ever made. For this reason alone, many good men and women do not enter into politics.

37

Second, you would have to realize that normal life as you know and cherish it, would come to an abrupt end. Family life would be greatly sacrificed upon the altar of a vagabond life-style as you traveled about the country speaking to group after group of total strangers. Each night you would sleep in a different bed, only to rise to a grueling repeat performance the next day.

Third, your reputation would suffer. No matter how spotless your character or how pure your words, you would wake morning after morning only to *"bear to hear the truth you'd spoken, twisted by knaves to make a trap for fools."* (Kipling) These we refer to as headlines. Many people would no longer look at you as a real person with real feelings, but rather as an object of political expediency, to be misrepresented and abused at will; and maybe even shot at. Then, in spite of all this, (as if that were not enough) every day you would face the gnawing reality of knowing that your chances of success were very slim at best. Doesn't sound too pleasant does it?

Yet, every four years this is exactly what a handful of prominent Americans face. We call them presidential candidates. Although these people may seem different than normal Americans, the truth is that they are just individual citizens like you and me. Some came from affluent backgrounds while others came from very obscure beginnings. Some are successful businessmen and women while others came through the ranks of political service. Whatever their differences, however, they all share one thing in common; they all have to stop and consider what a race for the White House would do to their personal lives.

So again, taking all these things into consideration, what would your answer be? Would your love of country compel you to say yes? Would your sense of patriotic duty demand that you make the sacrifice? Would you have what it takes to even try?

Fortunately, most of us will never have to face such a decision. No one will ever ask us to run for president. Nonetheless, I am asking you to make the *same kind* of commitment to your country. I am asking you to make the *same kind* of conscious decision that every presidential candidate must make. I am asking you to make a total commitment to God on behalf of your country. I am asking you to consciously dedicate yourself to the struggle for our nation's future.

Do not misunderstand me. I am not asking you to join a political party. I am not asking you to become a candidate or to back a candidate. I am not even asking you to become involved in the American political process. (As I've stated before, this we should do because we are good Americans.) Instead, I am asking you to make a difference by the sheer spiritual force of your prayers. I am asking that we join together in a force of one to pray that God will heal and bless our nation; that he will give us godly leaders from the county courthouse to the nation's White House. I am not asking for you to seek to occupy Air Force One, but to sanctify it and its next occupant by becoming a part of Prayer Force One.

Even though you are not being asked to make a run for the White House, each one of us must make the same kind of commitment that a presidential candidate must make. Why should we do less? By this I mean that each of us must make a conscious decision to be a part, to do our part, with no less fervency than if we ourselves were the candidate. Thinking this way helps us to focus on the importance that each individual plays in the process of saving our nation. Therefore, in keeping with our theme, let's consider what a winning presidential campaign must have and then draw some parallel conclusions.

I. A Winning Candidate

First, the candidate would have to make a personal decision to run. No candidate - no campaign. It is as simple as that! Everything begins with the individual. Everything rises and falls on leadership. That's the way God made it. Even the LORD himself said, *"I sought for a man among them, that should make up the hedge, and stand in the gap before me for the land, that I should not destroy it: but I found none."* (Ezekiel 22:30) Finding good leadership has always been the problem. But where do we find such men and women?

In his book, *A Different Drummer*, long time Reagan aide, Michael Deaver tells an interesting story. He said that Ronald Reagan's simple belief that Americans could become anything they wanted, absolutely drove him crazy. Then one day it dawned on him that

Ronald Reagan sincerely believed this because of his own humble beginnings. You and I must realize that *great people are really just ordinary people who believe great things*. Therefore, great people are everywhere. America is full of great people. Among these are people who believe that prayer changes things; even the destiny of nations. Perhaps you are one of them. Like many others, you are gravely concerned about our country, but, thank God, you have not given up on her.

> ## *"Great people are just ordinary people who believe great things."*

When Ronald Reagan lost the Republican nomination to Gerald Ford in 1976, he said something very interesting to his backers. He simply said:

> *"Don't become cynical. Remember what you were willing to do, and then remember that there are millions of other Americans that feel the same way you do. . .* (voice breaking) *. . . that want America to remain that shining city on a hill."*

Though few, if any, understood it then, we now know that Reagan's successful campaign for the White House began on that night, the night of his greatest defeat. The point that I'm trying to make is this, a committed candidate is the most important element to winning; especially when that candidate understands that there are others who are willing to sacrifice for the same lofty goals.

This is why I am not just writing a book about prayer, but about *committing* to prayer as part of a committed whole. I do this because I have come to believe something great. I believe that God meant what He said in II Chronicles 7:14. Therefore, I believe that America can still be saved. I know that many others believe this too. What I'm proposing is that we join together to build *a spiritual prayer force* for America. This, I believe, is God's vision for Prayer Force One. If God's people unite in sincere and humble prayer, there is no force on earth that can stop us, for the God who answers prayer is greater than all!

II. A Winning Message

The second thing that a successful presidential campaign must have is a message of hope. People must be convinced that the candidate offers a better tomorrow, and a way to fix the mistakes of the past. No one is going to throw away their vote on a man or woman who has no solutions for the problems that we face.

Our message is a simple one, and is based upon the sincere promises of the Bible. We believe that our nation is great because we have been God-blessed; that *"God shed His grace on thee"* (*America The Beautiful*). We believe that we must continue to acknowledge the hand of God, upon America, and that a national reaffirmation of this is vital for our nation's continued prosperity.

After 9/11, Major League Baseball added a new feature to their regular games. During the seventh inning stretch, the teams began inviting different people to sing Irving Berlin's famous World War II era song, *"God Bless America."* This is the kind of spiritual acknowledgment that serves to rebuild the soul of an ailing nation. This kind of expression cannot be taken away by silly judges with wrong-headed agendas, who seek to socially engineer a godless America. This is the kind of thing that we must work for and pray for, because this is the kind of thing that honors the only One that can truly bless America, God Almighty.

Ours is a message of hope, which is based on rebuilding a sense of individual accountability coupled with the power of faith and prayer. This is the message that America needs to hear today. I predict that the next great movement to sweep across America will be a spiritual one. I believe that we will either reaffirm our faith in God as a people, or we will turn our back on the One who has blessed us. We will either enter into a new era of Divine blessings or we will condemn our children to a fate worse than anything that communism ever thought of. This is the campaign that we are now engaged in. Our message is to rally the faithful and to call our nation to spiritual action; the greatest of which is prayer.

III. A Winning Strategy

The third thing necessary to a winning bid for the White House is a well thought out, well-defined campaign strategy. This strategy must include a plan to get the message out, and then to recruit and mobilize faithful volunteers. There is something exhilarating about becoming a part of something really great. This is why we must recognize the need to call our fellow Americans to band together in prayer. Many, if not most, of the great revivals of the Bible began in this manner. (See Nehemiah 1:3-4 with 4:9. See also II Chronicles 30:1 with verses 18-20 and verses 26-27, etc.)

Imagine 7 prayer warriors becoming 70, and 70 becoming 700. Imagine that 700 becoming 7,000, for as God said to Elijah, *"I have reserved to myself seven-thousand men, who have not bowed the knee to the image of Baal."* (I Kings 19:18 and Romans 11:4) Imagine such a core group forming the backbone of Prayer Force One! And, we need not stop here. Imagine this 7,000 becoming 70,000, 700,000, and even 7 million praying Americans on the Sunday before the next presidential election. We will not know if we do not try. Now, you begin to envision our goal for a national *"Prayer Force One Sunday"* to be held on the Sunday before the next presidential election. (And every national election thereafter.) This is the very real potential of Prayer Force One.

Our strategy is for waging spiritual warfare with spiritual weapons, with a spiritual victory in view. For too long we have sought to win our nations battles as if they were but political contests. They are not. They are spiritual battles. *"For we wrestle not against flesh and blood, but against principalities, against powers, against the rulers of the darkness of this world, against spiritual wickedness in high places."* (Ephesians 6:12) Such warfare demands the use of spiritual weapons. This is what the Bible means when it says, *"For the weapons of our warfare are not carnal, but mighty through God to the pulling down of strong holds."* (II Corinthians 10:4) This is also what the Bible means when it extols the exploits of the people, *"Who through faith subdued kingdoms, wrought righteousness, obtained promises, and stopped the mouths of lions."* (Hebrews 11:33)

Allow me to give a personal example. Years ago, when I was headed to Australia as a church planter, we and others were denied entry by the government of the labor party under the leadership of

Goff Whitlam. On November 10, 1975, I was in Atlanta, Georgia for a meeting. After the service, at about nine o'clock P.M., I decided to pray all night that God would do whatever was necessary to open the doors to Australia. As the sun rose the next morning, I picked up a newspaper to read that Australia's Governor General, Sir John Kerr, had dismissed the Whitlam government and called for new parliamentary elections. While I was praying all night on November tenth in America, it was already the morning of November eleventh in Australia. To this day, that event remains hugely controversial in Australia's political history. (You may look it up on the internet by entering a Google search on either Goff Whitlam or Malcolm Fraser) I believe that God answered my prayers even while I prayed. I believe that a kingdom was subdued for the glory of Christ that night. After that, many Christian ministers were once again allowed into Australia. This was a great lesson for me and I have never forgotten it. Prayer will work for America too!

Can you imagine a national prayer meeting on the Sunday before the next presidential election in which millions are participating. Imagine prayer meetings going on in churches all across America, on college campuses, and in living rooms, in apartment houses and farmhouses, in prisons and hospitals and even in the White House. Why not?! This is exactly what we propose for November 2, 2008, and before every subsequent national election thereafter. Richard Nixon talked about *"the silent majority"*. Jerry Falwell talked about *"the moral majority"*. Today, the need of the hour is for *"a praying majority"*! Teddy Roosevelt talked about *"a square deal"* for America, F.D.R. talked about *"the new deal"*, we however are talking about *"the real deal"*, for *"God ruleth in the kingdom of men, and that He appointeth over it whomsoever He will."* (Daniel 5:21) We must return to this reality, and like the words on our Washington's revolutionary naval flag, we must make, *"An Appeal To Heaven."*

6¢ U.S. POSTAGE — AN APPEAL TO HEAVEN — WASHINGTON'S CRUISERS FLAG 1775

IV. A Winning Financial Plan

Every winning presidential campaign must also have proper funding, the lack of which has ended many an otherwise good campaign. We are not so naive as to believe that Prayer Force One can be successful without proper funding too. We and our supporters must underwrite the expenses of this great endeavor. We must not only seek out and obtain major donors to sponsor our work, but the people themselves must undergird our united efforts by many small and continuous donations.

To this end, we have established *The Friends of Prayer Force One*, as part of our internet presence. Although Prayer Force One was born out of a small country church, that does not mean that people from all across America cannot have a part in it. On the contrary, we will not succeed without it. For those who wish to have a part, please go to our web site at: <www.PrayerForceOne.com>. We are not the least bit bashful in asking for your help; and may the LORD bless you for what you do. We have a Prayer Force One windshield decal of our logo for all who do.

V. A Winning Objective

Finally, a winning presidential campaign must have a tangible objective. Just as sure as each candidate wants to win the White House, even so, we also have an objective in view. We are asking the LORD to give us godly leaders. Our prayer is that Biblical virtue and family values might once again prevail in our nation. We desire God's favor and heaven's blessings that our children might grow up in a society of peace and purity. The Bible says, *"Righteousness exalteth a nation: but sin is a reproach to any people."* (Proverbs 14:34)

You see, it *does* matter who is in office. The Bible says *"When the righteous are in authority, the people rejoice: but when the wicked beareth rule, the people mourn."* (Proverbs 29:2) Our contention is that we have almost left God completely out of the equation. In a sense, many believers have, in effect, become *"Christian humanists"* as it were, because we have often relied upon our own political influence rather than an appeal to the God of heaven. Again, our agenda is a spiritual one not a political one. As an American, get as involved as you wish, but do not forget that all is vain without the blessings of God. The Bible says:

> *"Except the LORD build the house, they labor in*
> *vain that build it: except the LORD keep the city, the*
> *watchman waketh but in vain."* (Psalm 127:1)

Prayer Force One desires a person of God's own choosing in the White House, and in all other public offices. However, we, as a ministry, are not engaged in political campaigning or in the effort to persuade voters. Every American is free to do this on their own or as a part of some other effort or organization. We believe that the only sure way to obtain this objective is to pray for *God* to put such people into office. After all, praying *is* the churches' job! Jesus said, *"My house shall be called of all nations the house of prayer."* (Mark 11:17) In fact, the Bible specifically instructs the church to pray for all those in authority, that we may lead peaceful, godly lives. (Again, see I Timothy 2:1-3) This is why Prayer Force One born as a ministry of a local New Testament Church. However, other Christians as well as other churches are encouraged to partner with us in this great ecclesiastically inspired endeavor.

What Is Your Answer?

So, back to our original question. No, you are not being asked to run for president of the United States. However I *am* asking you to be just as committed to your country as if *you* were. And why not? It's your country too! Why not make the same kind of commitment by becoming a part of Prayer Force One?

The Prayer Force One Commitment
"I _____ do this
day dedicate myself to praying for revival in America,
and to encourage others to pray as well. I will also pray
for Ed Moore and the ministry of Prayer Force One."
Date:_____

Please let us know of your commitment by writing us, or by responding via our web site. Thank you for your prayers and support!

"Now is the time for all good men
to come to the aid of their country."

Chapter Five
A Plan For Uniting America's Praying Majority

Someone once said that every new idea goes through three stages of reaction from others. The first is, *"That's crazy, it'll never work."* The second is, *"It might work, but it's not worth doing."* The third is, *"I've always said that it was a good idea!"*

Well, the idea that we are talking about in this book is a good one. It is so good, in fact, that God is the one who thought it up! The promise of II Chronicles 7:14 is a Divine promise. However, like a generous check, you can only enjoy it if you take it to the bank and cash it. In II Chronicles 7:14, God has given us the right plan for saving America. The only real question remaining is how long will it be before we wake up and take it to the bank of heaven?

I'm reminded of the story of a farmer involved in a wreck when somebody rear ended his John Deere tractor on a country highway. It seems that a crowd had gathered around while a woman kneeled over the injured man. About this time, a brash young man came pushing his way through the crowd. As he pushed the woman back he was heard to say, *"Let me take over, I've had first-aid training."* After about thirty seconds, the woman gently tapped the young man on the shoulder, and said, *"When you get to the part of your training that says 'Call for a doctor,' - Here I am!"*

In much the same way, I believe God is simply waiting for us to realize our national folly and to re-acknowledge Him as the hope of our nation. Isn't it time that Christians wise up and realize that prayer is the God-ordained path to national healing? Isn't it also interesting that our nation's moral woes began to skyrocket just after the Supreme

Court of America banned prayer in our public schools? It seems we have tried everything else to save America. We've tried politics. We've fought wars. Many have staked their trust in Wall Street. However, our country seems to keep right on sliding down the path of moral decline.

Evangelical Christians have even stepped up and re-shouldered their civic duties and responsibilities as demonstrated by the emergence of what the press calls *"the Christian right"*. I applaud everyone involved. I have been one of them; even to the point of running for and holding public office. I got so involved, that I went on to serve as a delegate to one of the national presidential nominating conventions. But is it possible, that even in all of this, we have simply become *"Christian activists"*, while failing to realize the rightful place of prayer in the process?

For those who agree, let me say that we must get just as serious about prayer as any of these other courses of action. However, if we are to succeed, we must have a united prayer strategy. This is where you and I and Prayer Force One come in. By now, you have a pretty good idea of what Prayer Force One is all about. What many of you are no doubt saying is this. *"OK, I'm in agreement, but what are you asking me to do? How can I help?"* Here is what we propose.

The National Prayer Force One Plan of Action

The time has come for individual Christians, denominations and ministries to unite together in a national call to prayer. There is room for all of us to work together, without compromising the uniqueness of any of us. We must come together in issuing this national call to prayer. In the following paragraphs, I have outlined a plan that we are asking you to endorse, promote and become involved in. It may be that at some future time, emerging prayer leaders may decide to meet in a *National Prayer Summit* to further refine a national prayer strategy. Until then, I propose the following actions.

I. Agree On A Date.

In order to meet the *"if"* requirement of II Chronicles 7:14, we must first recognize the need to *organize* a national prayer meeting. To do this, it naturally follows that we must select and embrace an agreeable date for this to occur. However, not just any date will do. We must select a date that will capture the focus and imagination of all Americans. What better day could there be, than to pray on the Sunday before the next U. S. Presidential election? Just as the name, *"Prayer Force One"* arrests the attention and captures the imagination of all who hear of it, even so, the phrase, *"the Sunday before the next Presidential election"* says it all. I believe this is the right date for three reasons.

1. As Americans, we need special wisdom from heaven before selecting our national leaders. After all, it *does* matter who is in office! The Bible says, *"When the righteous are in authority, the people rejoice: but when the wicked beareth rule, the people mourn."* (Proverbs 29:2) Although Prayer Force One is not a political organization or movement; and although we do not endorse candidates or political parties, we do see the need for Divine guidance as we select our leaders.

This is especially true when you consider that the 2008 presidential contest will not have an incumbent. The White House will be empty where the future is concerned. For this reason alone, there will be a much higher degree of public awareness and interest in the 2008 election. By aligning our prayer date to coincide with this great contest, we will be able to take advantage of America's heightened consciousness. What better day could we possibly pray than on the Sunday before we elect our next president? Proximity to the election does not make us political, but rather spiritually wise. Add to this the fact that our Congressionally approved *National Day of Prayer* is as far removed from election day as it could possibly be. (Exactly six months removed!)

If one studies the prayer life of Jesus Christ, you will discover that His all-night prayer vigils were always just prior to some great decision or event in His life. Isn't this compelling reason for us to pray before our national elections?

2. Americans think in terms of elections. Every four years we elect our President. Every two years we elect our Congress. It's simply American. Therefore, it's natural for our people to focus on that date. Although the actual date of the next presidential election is November

4th, which makes our first proposed prayer date Sunday, November 2nd, you really don't have to remember all this. By simply saying that we are all going to pray on the Sunday before the next presidential election, you've said it all.

Prayer, you see, is a very abstract thing for many people. Real, yes, but abstract too. However, by focusing on a very concrete and easily remembered day, we help people to identify with, and participate in, a very abstract idea. Wisdom is justified of her children.

3. What better day to pray than on Sunday, when churches all across America are already meeting? Jesus said, *"My house shall be called the house of prayer."* (Matthew 21:13) Therefore, nothing out of the ordinary needs to be organized. All that is left to do is to recruit participants and coordinate the unity of the event. Can you imagine such a Sunday? Would this not be pleasing to God?

II. Recruit people to pray as part of Prayer Force One.

Again, to meet the *"if"* requirements of II Chronicles 7:14, *people* participation is the key. All else is vain if the *people* do not join together in prayer. Therefore, we must recruit *people* to this great cause. This is where organization becomes necessary. Although Prayer Force One is more of a concept than an organization, it is nevertheless important to success that we recruit and organize. *People* can read and agree with this book until the cows come home, but until each one makes a personal commitment to become a part, their participation can neither be counted on nor coordinated. For this reason, we ask each and every one of you to consider doing these four things.

1. Make A Holy Vow To God. Vow to personally do what II Chronicles 7:14 says. A holy commitment to God is the key. We must each humble ourselves before God. We often forget that this is the first requirement of II Chronicles 7:14. After all, prayer without humility is an exercise in spiritual arrogance. We must each confess our sins, and the sins of our nation. We must each ask God to forgive us, and ask God to heal our land. Along with this, we ask each of you to make a solemn commitment to participate in the first, *National Prayer Force One Sunday*, to be held on November 2, 2008. It may be that the only way you can participate is to pray in your own home. Regardless of how you choose to participate, let us know of your commitment to pray by going to our web site and clicking on the *"YES, I'll Pray"* button. Please fill out the information requested so that we might keep you informed as to the progress of the Prayer Force One effort. Please stop and do this now. Our internet address is *www.PrayerForceOne.com*. If you do not have internet access, you may write to us at:

Prayer Force One
P.O. Box 270
Newalla, OK 74857

2. Pray For The Ministry Of Prayer Force One. There is much to do and many answers to prayer that must be received long before *Prayer Force One Sunday.* We must earnestly work at uniting *"America's Praying Majority"*. Pray every day for the ministry of Prayer Force One. Pray for Sandy and I as we lead this great, spirit-led ministry, as well as for all the dedicated members of our staff. You are encouraged to pray for us as part of your daily prayer time, or as part of our daily White House prayer meeting. (See Chapter Six)

3. Start A *PF-1 Prayer Wing* In Your Home Or Church. A *Prayer Wing* is simply a prayer group which is dedicated to praying for revival in America in association with Prayer Force One. We are currently developing all kinds of support materials that will soon be added to those already available to you from our web site. Some of these are listed in the back of this book as well. To find out more about starting a *PF-1 Prayer Wing*, see Appendix A on page 233. Please remember, no one else can do what you alone can do.

4. Support Prayer Force One. Every ministry must have the financial resources to fulfill its purpose. We are asking everyone to do what they can. A hundred people giving ten dollars a month is just as effective as one person giving one thousand dollars. If thousands participate, all of the needs will be met, including a very costly television campaign. Visit our web site or use the address given above if God leads you to contribute to this ministry. When you do, you will receive a colorfast window decal of our beautiful Prayer Force

One emblem. All gifts are tax deductible.

III. Re-educate Americans About How God Deals With Nations.

Somewhere during America's "*devolution*" into a humanistic society, our citizens have forgotten what the Bible says concerning God and nations. Many Americans are also unaware of our rich spiritual heritage. If left unchecked, this ignorance will become terminal. The Bible contains a very solemn, stern and sobering warning to us as God says:

> "*My people are destroyed for lack of knowledge:*
> *because thou hast rejected knowledge, I also will reject*
> *thee. . .seeing thou hast forgotten the law of thy God,*
> *I will also forget thy children.*"   (Hosea 4:6)

If America is to be saved, we must remember what the prophet Daniel told Nebuchadnezzar, King of Babylon: "*That the living may know that the most High ruleth in the kingdom of men.*" (Daniel 4:17) Yes, there is a God in heaven, and this benevolent God deals with nations just as he deals with individuals. The Bible promises: "*Blessed is the nation whose God is the LORD.*" (Psalm 33:12) However, the same Bible also warns us that: "*The wicked shall be turned into hell, and all the nations that forget God.*" (Psalm 9:17)

In an effort to preserve this essential knowledge of the Bible and our spiritual heritage, we have developed Part II of this book entitled: *The Message Of Prayer Force One*. This section contains a number of Bible studies concerning our nation, its heritage, and the power of prayer. These studies are designed to be used in many different ways and in many different settings. I have listed nine possible uses for your consideration.

1. They can be used in personal and family devotional times.

2. They can be used by pastors as a basis for sermons and sermon illustrations.

3. They can be used as a Sunday School curriculum.

4. They can be used as the curriculum for a weekly home Bible study group.

5. They can be used as a seven-week study course for both men's and ladies' Bible study groups.

6. They can be used for youth groups.

7. They can be used as educational devotionals for work-based prayer groups, etc.

8. They can be used as patriotic devotionals in the many congressional and state legislative prayer groups across America.

9. They can be used in the White House Bible study/prayer group, not to mention by the President himself.

The important thing to consider is how you can use these sound Bible devotionals to teach these Bible truths in *your* own world. Again, Appendix A on page 233 describes how to start a Prayer Force One, *Prayer Wing* in your home, church or place of business. I believe that such a prayer group will be quite enjoyable and edifying, not to mention how important it may prove to be for the nation.

IV. Get Involved In Promoting Prayer For America.

In addition to the four main commitments listed above, here is a list of twenty-one thoughtful ways that praying Americans can get more involved in promoting the ministry of Prayer Force One. Some of them have already been mentioned. Certainly no one can do them all, but as you look the list over, place a check mark by those suggestions that you could possibly do.

__**1.** Set aside a time each day to pray for your country. At the time of this writing, our web site has a direct link to the White House, allowing you to have a time of quiet prayer in a different room of the White House each day. Simply go to our web site and click on our White House prayer link and follow directions. We encourage you to take advantage of this as long as these rooms are available to us. If you will do this for seven to ten days, you will develop a new habit of praying for your country and its leaders. The next chapter is entirely devoted to this very unique prayer meeting.

__**2.** Put Prayer Force One decals and postcards everywhere to remind you to pray. Put one on your bathroom mirror, and another on your refrigerator. Put a sticker on the back of your car window and at your place of employment. We all need reminders to pray.

__**3.** Use Prayer Force One prayer reminders not only to remind you to pray, but as door openers to share the need for national prayer with your family, friends and co-workers. On our web site, there is a link from which you may order coffee cups, mouse pads, golf shirts, etc. We also have ministry decals and post cards available from our regular home page.

__**4.** Pass our Prayer Force One postcards out to everyone you meet. These are beautifully produced and really get results. It is amazing how people do keep these, and how many actually visit our web site because of them.

__**5.** Forward our e-mails and web articles to your family and friends on a regular basis. They are each designed so that you can do this with ease. These articles and e-mails have a life of their own, and, like the energizer bunny, they just keep going and going.

__**6.** Start a Prayer Force One *Prayer Wing* (prayer group) in your church or home. Use the lessons in Part II to facilitate discussion. Use the guidelines in Appendix A to find suggestions on how to start a Prayer Force One *Prayer Wing*.

__**7.** Encourage your youth pastor to start a Prayer Force One prayer group among your youth, and/or to use the Prayer Force One Bible studies in your youth group.

__**8.** Encourage your ladies' ministry coordinator to use the Prayer Force One Bible Studies in the ladies' meetings. This can be quite different than what your ladies have been used to.

__**9.** Encourage your men's ministry coordinator to do the same thing. Men especially need to stand up and pray for their nation.

__**10.** Start a Prayer Force One *Prayer Wing* at your work place and/ or use the PF-1 Bible studies during work-based devotional times.

__**11.** Make available or give away as many copies of this book, *Prayer Force One Across America,* as you can. Get them into the hands of your pastor, youth leader, newspaper editor, etc. We have great discounts when ordered by the case or in bulk lots. See our web site or use the order form at the back of this book.

__**12.** Ask your local bookstore manager to carry our book, *Prayer Force One: Across America*, and then tell your friends where they can be purchased.

__**13.** Talk about Prayer Force One on call-in talk radio, etc.

__**14.** Use our special church bulletin inserts. They are designed to be used in this manner, and fit very nicely inside the standard 8-1/2 by 11 folded church bulletin. These can be downloaded from our web site and then copied. No permission is required for you to do this. This is probably the most effective way to promote prayer for national revival that we know of. More is accomplished with less effort than almost anything else your church could do.

__**15.** During special meetings in your church such as revival meetings, vacation Bible school and youth camps, give special emphasis to the ministry of Prayer Force One. Give out a Prayer Force One postcard to everyone in attendance, and make Prayer Force One prayer reminders available to all who want them.

__**16.** College students should pass out Prayer Force One literature on campus and advertise the formation of a Prayer Force One prayer group on campus. For colleges that already have an established Christian presence on campus, ask to share the vision of Prayer Force One to those who attend. Christian student unions are great for this.

__**17.** U.S. military units also have many opportunities for embracing and promoting the work of Prayer Force One.

__**18.** Pastors can not only use Prayer Force One materials in their own church, but are encouraged to share the vision and materials at denominational meetings and pastoral fellowships. Why not invite someone from the Prayer Force One speakers bureau to come and present the ministry of Prayer Force One?

__**19.** Encourage your home town editor to carry our Prayer Force One syndicated column in your local newspaper. See chapter seven to find out more about our syndicated column, or see our web site for more information.

__**20.** Evangelists, unencumbered ministers and retired people can have a tremendous impact by becoming a certified independent Prayer Force One representative. Evangelists, your ministry could become an even greater blessing to America and be greatly enhanced by presenting the ministry of Prayer Force One in your meetings. Have a special Prayer Force One night in your meetings. One of the great things is that you can conduct three different meetings at three different churches during a single week. Love offerings coupled with book table sales can help to meet your financial needs. Discounted materials are available to all certified, independent representatives.

When you become a certified independent Prayer Force One representative, you will be listed among the available speakers for your state or region on the Prayer Force One web site. You may expect to receive calls to come and present the Prayer Force One ministry to various churches and civic groups.

__21. Invite Prayer Force One to come to your area by organizing a Prayer Force One Rally or Crusade in your town or city. Under certain conditions, Prayer Force One will visit your city and appear at these one or two night meetings.

A Modern Parable, Born From A Personal Testimony

Sandy and I have six wonderful children. Randi, is our fourth child and our third daughter. Sandy and I always thought that Randi would be the child that would stay closest to home. How wrong we were. She has been on mission trips to Romania, Italy and the Czech Republic. Several years ago she married a fine young preacher and at the time of this writing, they are preparing to graduate from California Baptist University in Riverside California, in preparation for the ministry.

When Randi was very little, we were traveling about the country as an evangelist. We pulled a thirty-foot travel trailer behind our car in order to keep some semblance of a home life. Since Randi was the youngest of four at the time, we had little room left in the trailer for her to sleep. To solve this problem, we simply tucked her into a little overhead cupboard above our bed. Each night she would hang her little arm down to me and I would hold her hand and sing and pray with her until she drifted off to sleep.

Randi is all grown up now. Not long ago, just before Christmas of 2004, Randi called home from California with bad news. She told us that she had several hard lumps growing on the back of her neck. She had been experiencing severe head aches and nausea. It seems this had been a growing concern for some time. Finally, Randi went to several doctors in California. The third doctor told her he thought she had Lymphoma cancer and told her that she ought to return home to be with family as she pursued further treatment.

When Randi and her husband, Jonathan, returned home near Christmas, three doctors collaborated over an MRI which revealed three large growths on or near her spinal cord. They feared the worse. They concurred with the doctors in California that all signs pointed to cancer. A biopsy was scheduled to take place right after Christmas.

When Sandy and I heard the news, we both wept and prayed. I went to the altar of the church where I serve as pastor and wept before the Lord. I reminded God that Sandy and I had given each of our children, including Randi, to Him at birth. I told Him that if He wanted her, I would not argue, and then laid my earnest prayer for her healing before His throne. In the days which followed, Christian friends from fourteen states and seven countries on four continents were praying for Randi.

On the night before Randi was to go in for the biopsy, I could not sleep. I was up and down for a good part of the night; first praying, then reading the Bible. I made confession, and humbled myself before the LORD. God knows. Sometime in the wee hours of the morning, my pillow wet with tears, I lifted my hand in the still darkness and said, *"Dear God, do you remember how my little Randi held her hand out years ago because she needed to know Daddy was near? Well Lord, I'm asking you to hold my daughter's hand right now, and Lord, I'm asking you to heal her completely. Would you please do this for me?"* I tell you the truth, in that moment, a great peace came over my soul and I knew beyond a doubt that God had heard our prayers, and granted our request.

I telephoned Randi and Jonathan and told them that I believed God had heard our prayers and that all would turn out right. The next morning, our twenty-one-year-old baby went bravely through the door with a fine Christian doctor as the family prepared to wait.

Then, about ten minutes later, Randi returned with her doctor. *"So quick?"* Sandy asked.

"Mamma, we've got great news!" Randi cried.

The doctor then said, *"Well, I don't quite know what to say. All week long, I prayed that God would give me wisdom of how to tell a beautiful, twenty-one-year-old Christian girl that she had lymphoma cancer. But this morning all I can say is that the lumps are completely gone! I cannot biopsy the growths because there are no lumps to biopsy!"*

As you can imagine, we all rejoiced and cried and praised the LORD! Later that day I returned to the dark and quiet altar of my church. I thanked my God, who had healed my daughter through Christ our Savior. Then. . . I worshipped Him.

Beloved, this same God can heal our hurting land. All that is needed is for us to collectively lift our hearts to Him in humble, penitent prayer. Somewhere in the darkness of this present hour, there is a God in heaven who is willing to listen and heal our land. But we must first call our nation to prayer. Will you join me? Will you help me in this great cause? The next chapter will present something that you can do on a daily basis that will surely help to make a difference.

Requirements For Using The Prayer Force One Name & Logo

The name, *Prayer Force One*, and its logo are trademarks of the Prayer Force One ministry. While we encourage the formation of Prayer Force One groups, it must be understood that in order to protect the integrity of our ministry and its objectives, we maintain certain requirements of those who use the name or its logo. We list some of the basic ones below. The following requirements are subject to any current prevailing revisions, which are posted on our web site.

1. Prayer Force One is a Christian ministry that supports and defends Biblically-based family values. Our simple *Statement of Faith and Values* is posted on our web site. Those who use our name and logo must be in agreement with this statement.

2. While Christians may use the name Prayer Force One, no one may present themselves as a *Certified Representative* of Prayer Force One unless they are so authorized by Prayer Force One Headquarters.

3. Only one official web site shall present itself as representing Prayer Force One on the World Wide Web, nor shall any bank accounts be maintained apart from the home office unless written authorization is obtained from Prayer Force One headquarters.

4. Prayer Force One is a prayer ministry and does not endorse political parties or candidates. While our supporters are free to become involved in the political process as Americans, none may use the organization, its name, or its logo in support of or in the endorsement of any political candidate or party.

5. Prayer Force One is an ecclesiastical ministry. All donations are tax deductible. Prayer Force One will mail a year-end acknowledgment to each donor, containing the total contributions made by that contributor.

"*I exhort therefore, that, first of all, supplications, prayers, intercessions, and giving of thanks, be made for all men; for kings, and for all that are in authority; that we may lead a quiet and peaceable life in all godliness and honesty.*"

(I Timothy 2:1-2)

Chapter Six
Join Us For Daily Prayer In The White House

As you know by now, Prayer Force One is promoting two great prayer events. The first, is to be the culmination of all our efforts in a great day of national prayer on the Sunday before the next presidential election. (And before every national election thereafter.) This is known as *National Prayer Force One Sunday*, and will take place on Sunday, November 2, 2008.

The second great prayer event is an ongoing daily prayer meeting in the White House.

"In the White House?" you ask.

Yes, in the White House! Through the wonders of technology, anyone can now enjoy a beautiful 360-degree tour of the various rooms in the White House. (Courtesy of the White House.)

At Prayer Force One Headquarters, we have taken this great privilege to a new and spiritual level by organizing a prayer meeting in a different room of the White House each day of the week. You are encouraged to join us in this daily prayer meeting by going to our web site at: <www.PrayerForceOne.com> and clicking on the *"Pray In The White House"* button in the upper right hand corner. (Shown at right)

Of course, you will not see anyone else when you go to the chosen room of the day, but you will sense the presence of an ever growing number of praying Americans who join us in this *"virtual"* prayer meeting. In fact, this is one of the very few *"virtual"* experiences that actually transcends the limitations of a computer-generated *"virtual world"*. This is because a prayer meeting is anything but *"virtual"*. God knows what we are doing and why. I believe that He listens to our individual and collective prayers offered up during this time.

In fact, I must confess that my daily prayer time in the White House has become one of my favorite times of the day. First of all, I am quite sincere in the prayers that I send heavenward during this time. The Bible says; " *The whole land is made desolate, because no man layeth it to heart.*" (Jeremiah 12:11) I want God to know that there is at least one man in this country that has laid America to heart before the LORD. Thus, my prayer time in the White House has become very sacred to me. Just as I want my children to know that they have a praying daddy, so I want God to know that America has a preacher/politician, (take your pick, I've been both) praying for her!

Secondly, this time is precious to me because I sense the presence of others who also go to the White House to pray. Of course, our internet prayer logs confirm this, but it's more than that. There is a genuine sense of spiritual camaraderie, and that a national prayer meeting is indeed in progress. There is joy in knowing that there are many others, who, just like you, are daily visiting the Executive Mansion for the purpose of offering up prayers for our nation.

It does take a little time to form the habit, but if you will join our Prayer Force One, White House prayer meeting for seven to ten days, you too will find that you have formed a wonderful and fulfilling spiritual habit of praying for your country. In fact, if you are like me, I think you will find that this time becomes something that you look forward to each day. When this becomes a reality in your life, you will have truly become a part of America's Prayer Force, Prayer Force One! Of course, not everyone has daily access to a computer, and while you can join us in prayer without logging in to our daily prayer meeting, I think that you will agree that there is more of a kindred spirit when you actually go through the discipline of logging in for prayer each day.

Each day, when you log in, you will find instructions as to what room we are meeting in for that particular day. Likewise, you will also see what our particular prayer focus is for that day. From time to time you will log in to find a special request that everyone is asked to pray about for that day. Of course, in times of national crises, you will find very special instructions and requests too. Sometimes, you may log in to find a special prayer being offered by a special person or leader. At other times you may find a special praise report. Most generally, however, you will simply be asked to log in and pray. I want to encourage you to use this quiet time to pray for America and whatever else the LORD lays on your heart.

If you would like us to join you in a special prayer request, you may send it to us via our web site by clicking on the *"Spiritual Helps"* button and filling in the prayer request information. Each Sunday afternoon, I, or someone from our staff, will pray over all of the requests sent in for the week. We usually pray aboard Prayer Force One.

It is my sincere hope that you will not only take advantage of this great prayer effort, but that you will promote it among all of your praying friends. We have postcards about Prayer Force One, including one specifically designed to tell about our daily prayer meeting in the White House. You may order these from our web site. Once you have signed up to pray, you will occasionally receive an e-letter about our prayer objectives. We encourage you to forward these e-letters to all your family and friends.

Also, if for any reason, we lose access to the White House site to pray in, know that we will provide other national and patriotic venues for our daily prayer meeting. We could pray in the U.S. Capitol rotunda, or at Mount Rushmore, or in Independence Hall in Philadelphia, or in the Old North Church in Boston, or even in the Grand Canyon! (We may occasionally do this anyway!) The point is that we can pray together, and that our prayers can make a difference. However, we can only inform you of our activities if you sign up to pray. You will only have to do this once. (Unless there is a change in your information.) After that, you will simply need to log in, using your e-mail address to participate. All information will be kept confidential and used only for this purpose. We will never ask for any financial information.

For those who maintain their own web site, (Churches, Businesses, individuals, etc.) we have developed the button shown at left, which you are welcome to use on your own site. At the click of a button, both you and your web site patrons will be able to join us in our daily prayer meeting in the White House. To download this feature, just go to our web site, click on this button and follow directions.

Twenty-Six Guardians of Prayer

Allow me to close this chapter with this amazing true story, told by a missionary home on furlough to his home church in Michigan.

"While serving at a small field hospital in Africa, every two weeks I traveled by bicycle through the jungle to a nearby city for supplies. This was a journey of two days and required camping overnight at the halfway point. On one of these journeys, I arrived in the city where I planned to collect money from a bank, purchase medicine, and supplies, and then begin my two-day journey back to the field hospital. Upon arrival in the city, I observed two men fighting, one of whom had been seriously injured. I treated him for his injuries and at the same time talked to him about the Lord.

Two weeks later I repeated my journey. Upon arriving in the city, I was approached by the young man I had treated. He told me that he had known I carried money and medicines. He said, 'Some friends and I followed you into the jungle, knowing you would camp overnight. We planned to kill you and take your money and drugs. But just as we were about to move into your camp, we saw that you were surrounded by twenty-six armed guards.'

At this I laughed and said that I was certainly all-alone in that jungle camp site. The young man pressed the point, however, and said, 'No sir, I was not the only person to see the guards, my friends also saw them, and we all counted them. It was because of those guards that we were afraid and left you alone.'

At this point in the sermon, one of the men in the congregation jumped to his feet and interrupted the missionary and asked if he could tell him the exact day this happened. The missionary told the congregation the date, and the man who interrupted told him this story:

'On the night of your incident in Africa, it was morning here and I was preparing to go play golf. I was about to putt when I felt the urge to pray for you. In fact, the urging of the Lord was so strong, I called men in this church to meet with me here in the sanctuary to pray for you. Would all of those men who met with me on that day stand up?' The men who had met together to pray that day stood up. The missionary wasn't concerned with who they were, he was too busy counting how many men he saw. There were twenty-six."

America too, needs guardians of prayer. You will find an ever-growing number of them meeting each day in the White House to pray. Why don't you join us? We're going there now. To join us simply go to our web site at <www.PrayerForceOne.com> and click on our *"Pray In The White House"* button at the upper right corner. We'll meet you there.

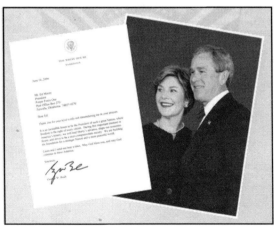

(Although our daily prayer meeting in the White House is neither authorized nor endorsed by the White House, On June 16, 2006, President George W. Bush wrote to express his gratitude for the prayers of those participating in the Prayer Force One ministry.)

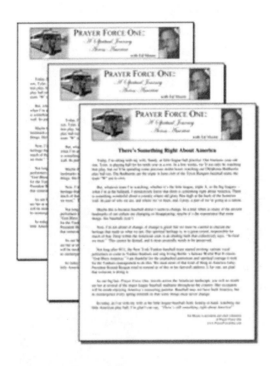

"In the multitude of people is the king's honour: but in the want of people is the destruction of the prince."

(Proverbs 14:28)

Chapter Seven
Our Syndicated Newspaper Column

There is great power in the written word. In spite of television and radio, readable words, whether electronically disseminated or printed in conventional form, will continue to propagate and preserve the great thoughts and collective wisdom of the ages. This is the first reason that we decided to write a weekly newspaper column.

Not only this, but we must also recognize that all governance is obtained or maintained by winning the minds of the people. The Bible says, *"In the multitude of people is the king's honor, but for want of people is the destruction of the prince."* (Proverbs 14:28) In today's terms, we would call this *"public support"*. The practical application of this is demonstrated by how a president's power to lead is affected by public approval ratings, which measure that public support. (You may rest assured that any politician who says that he doesn't pay attention to polls is currently down in his ratings.)

The battle for the hearts and minds of the people is always fought out in the media. Even the American Revolution was greatly influenced by a popular little pamphlet called *Common Sense*, and by the many Committees of Correspondence which existed throughout the colonies. It is no less true today. Although television and the movie industry are very influential in this regard, newspapers and radio remain the mainstay at the local level. In fact, these venues have staged a dramatic comeback in combatting the lopsided liberal influence exerted through television. This can be evidenced by the huge increase in the number of talk radio programs that have sprung up across America. Most of these are conservative in nature because they derive their support from prevailing local sentiment. There are many voices to be sure, and each voice is blended with others in the struggle for the heart of the masses. Just the same, it is the responsibility of each of us to do what we can to influence our society for good. This is the second reason that we decided to begin a syndicated newspaper column. We feel that it is simply our duty.

The power of the syndicated column is that it is repetitive. Newspaper columnists become trusted *"voices,"* if you please, in a world of competing *"noises"*. Once we become accustomed to a particular columnist or commentators views, we have a tendency to pay attention and have respect for their publicly expressed opinions. Not only this, but printed columns are regularly *"in their place"* and so tend to be repeatedly looked for and read by regular readers. For these reasons, I believe that syndicated newspaper columnists have an influence far beyond the seeming limitations of the printed page.

What Kind of Column?

Columns can present themselves in many types of formats. Some, like Dear Abby, Anne Landers and Billy Graham, are presented in a question and answer format. Some are in the form of humor, such as Erma Bombeck, etc. Still others are topical in nature, which specialize in a certain field of interest such as gardening or travel. A great many columnists depend on political commentary and opinions on current topics of public interest to keep them going. One of the greatest columnist's of all time, Will Rogers, became successful through a combination of trademark humor, travel and politics.

About Our Column

We gave a great deal of thought to the kind of column we wanted to write. After much prayer and thought, we decided that we too needed to combine several areas in a unique, one-of-a-kind column which, as you would expect, we call: *Prayer Force One: A Spiritual Journey Across America*. This column is unique because it combines several appealing formats into one. Allow me to list these.

1. First of all, like Billy Graham's column, *My Answer*, our column

makes no bones about being religious in nature. In each of our columns we always try to bring at least one passage of Scripture to bear upon the topic at hand. We feel that the greatest contribution that we can make is to reinforce the Christian influence, which has helped to weave the fabric of our national society. At the same time, we seek to encourage our readers spiritually, if we can. Because of its spiritual nature, we believe major city newspapers, magazines and hometown newspapers alike will find our column a welcome offering to meet the spiritual needs of their readers.

2. The second part of our unique mix is travel. Our commentaries are written as we travel about the country. So far, my wife, Sandy, and I have been to over forty states of the union. We are now involved in a forty-nine state tour aboard our bus, Prayer Force One. During this time we are meeting with as many of the governors and legislative leaders of the various states as possible. However, unlike normal travel columns, our stories are woven around the places and people we visit, instead of simply being about the destinations themselves. This is true traveling, full of history and human interest. This is travel as it should be - alive and full of spiritual adventure.

3. The third element of the mix is politics and people. Although our column is not political in the typical sense of trying to sway voters, it is political in the sense that America, itself, *is* a political environment. This country is full of candidates, contests, and issues. These, in the context of history, religion and geography make for an endless variety of interesting topics to write about. Here too, people are the key. In the days to come we hope to meet with and write about all kinds of people, from presidential candidates to spiritual and civic leaders; from the common everyday Americans, like me, to people of great national interest.

How To Learn More About Our Syndicated Column

Don't let the word syndicated scare you. That word simply means that our column is available for newspapers (or any other print medium) to purchase and print. In many cases, such columns and

features, (comic strips, etc.) are handled by a large *"syndicate"* which promotes and distributes the content to potential buyers, for a usual fifty percent fee, and often, ownership of other potential commercial uses. At this time, our column is privately syndicated as part of our non-profit ministry.

To learn more about our syndicated column, or to learn how a newspaper or magazine can subscribe and print this column, we have developed a special page on our web site. Interested parties should go to our web site at <www.PrayerForceOne.com> and then click on the button that reads *"Our Syndicated Column"*. This button is located on the right hand side of our home page, about half way down. (This button is pictured on the previous page.)

Once you have accessed our syndicated column page, you will see the series of buttons pictured to the left. Simply click on the button or buttons of interest to learn more. I might add that the *"Column Archive"* button contains many of our past columns. By reading some of these, you will get a pretty good idea of what one of our typical columns is like.

We have also included a short selection of past columns on the pages that follow. These will also give the reader an idea of what to expect. Not surprisingly, the first one included is about columnists.

What You Can Do to Help

In closing, allow me to encourage you to call your local editor and encourage him or her to carry our column in your hometown newspaper. When they do, be sure to write and let them know how much you appreciate being able to read the column on a regular basis. A little expressed appreciation goes a long way!

PRAYER FORCE ONE:
A Spiritual Journey Across America

with Ed Moore

My Heroes Have All Been Columnists

On our recent trip to California, we went by the ranch home of Will Rogers. Though he died 17 years before I was born, Will was my boyhood hero. In fact, I learned to spin a rope because of my admiration for this remarkable man. At the time of his death in 1935, Will Rogers was the number one Hollywood box-office attraction in the country, knocking down over $300,000 per film during the great depression. But for all of that, it was his newspaper column, *Will Rogers Says*, that made him the most popular man in America. As we toured his California ranch, it suddenly dawned on me that most all of my heroes have been columnists.

Almost everyone remembers that Ronald Reagan was a movie actor, spokesman for General Electric, and of course, President of the United States. But, what we often overlook is that Reagan was also a columnist and radio commentator. I was reminded of this as Sandy and I recently walked through the Reagan Presidential Library and saw an old record containing one of his radio commentaries. On the label was written: *"recorded for release on:____"* (place for a handwritten date).

Billy Graham is another good example. We all remember him as the enduring evangelist and *"Pastor to Presidents,"* but perhaps the greatest secret to his staying power has been his daily newspaper column, *My Answer*, which, for over 50 years, has reached over 20 million readers daily.

My point is that there is power in the written word. The Bible says, *"Where the word of a king is there is power."* (Ecclesiastes 8:4) Is it any wonder that the gospel of John begins with, *"In the beginning was the Word."*? (John 1:1) The third verse of the entire Bible begins with *"And God said. . ."* (Genesis 1:3) You might say that God himself was the first columnist. The only difference is that his writings are not just opinions. His words rule the universe!

This country of ours was founded upon God's *"column,"* if you please. President Ulysses S. Grant said, "That Bible, Sir, is the rock on which this republic rests." Every single U.S. president has taken the oath of office with his hand upon the Bible. When George Washington was sworn into office, he actually paused and kissed the Bible, which had been used in the ceremony.

There's not a lot wrong with America that couldn't be fixed, if we just went back to taking advice from the greatest columnist of all time. My heroes have almost all been columnists.

Ed Moore is President and Chief Columnist for Prayer Force One
www.PrayerForceOne.com

71

PRAYER FORCE ONE:
A Spiritual Journey
Across America

with Ed Moore

"I Need To Connect"

Although my preferred way of traveling is aboard our specially designed, greyhound-style motor coach, known as *Prayer Force One*, today I'm headed south to Fort Worth, Texas, aboard Amtrak's *Heartland Flyer*. The hostess at our Norman, Oklahoma station is a lady by the name of Danielle. In meeting her as I checked in, I explained to her that I was a minister on a national mission and sorely needed some time to have *"a date with my brain."*

"I'm overdue for that sort of thing too," she said wistfully. A few minutes later, as I waited for my train, I overheard her whispering, *"I need to connect. I've got to get connected."* Since she was speaking to herself, I hesitated, and then politely intruded by asking, *"What do you mean, 'I need to get connected.'?"* She looked up from her computer and said, *"Oh, I'm just trying to get on the Internet, and I can't get connected."* As a minister, I thought that she was hinting at a need for spiritual help. She sensed my misguided concern, and we both began to laugh. I told her that many times, people wouldn't just come out and ask for help. Yet sooner or later, we all sense that need to get *"connected"* or *"reconnected,"* as the case may be.

Later, while passing through the Arbuckle Mountains of south-central Oklahoma, we passed a bend in the Washita River. As I looked out, I saw an old severed pick-up truck bed with a ratty camper shell on it. There were some clothes hanging out to dry, and a Coleman cook stove in the midst of the trash that surrounded it. I was somewhat taken aback by this out-of-the-way hobo hut. There were no roads in or out, and no vehicle was in sight, yet, it was obvious that someone was living there.

As the Amtrak's horn sounded, I found myself wondering who could possibly be living in such a solitary place. Was it a forgotten man, a hermit by choice? Was it someone trying to escape the blows that life had dealt him? Or was it simply a hunter, or maybe a writer, like me, in need of some down time? Sometimes, I think we all need to get away from it all, in order to reconnect. Jesus once told his disciples, *"Come ye yourselves apart into a desert place, and rest a while, for there were many coming and going."* (Mark 6:31) One minister said that this meant, *"Come ye apart, lest ye come apart!"* Sometimes, we just need time to pray and to seek God's face. Perhaps we would all do well to listen to that still, small voice that says, *"I need to connect."* In pausing to listen, we might well find ourselves within earshot of heaven!

Ed Moore is President and Chief Columnist for Prayer Force One
www.PrayerForceOne.com

PRAYER FORCE ONE:
A Spritual Journey Across America

with Ed Moore

Give 'Em Heaven Harry!

Several months ago, Sandy, and I went to Independence, Missouri, to pick up a new generator for our bus, *Prayer Force One*. When we got there, we discovered that we were only a couple of miles from the Harry S. Truman Presidential Library, and homesite. Although Harry Truman was still president when I was born, (Eisenhower was president-elect, by just nine days) I soon discovered that I had a lot to learn about Harry.

Did you know that Harry Truman's early life was literally filled with failure? In 1916, he started a zinc mining company in northeast Oklahoma, but soon went broke. Then, he tried his hand in the oil fields of Kansas, but after running dry of investors, he sold his rights to an outfit which struck it rich. He had sold a field of gushers! At the conclusion of WWI, Harry and a war buddy went in as partners in a men's clothing store. In 1921, this too went belly-up.

As I was contemplating all of this, I couldn't help but ask, "How could a man with this kind of background become President of the United States?" The answer, of course, was Harry Truman's tenacity. He just wouldn't quit. Ten years behind a mule and plow had made Harry Truman tough. In the 1948 elections, absolutely no one, not even

his wife, Bess, thought that he could win re-election. Truman thought otherwise, and after one of the greatest whistle-stop campaigns in American history, he made the *Chicago Tribune*, as well as the rest of the world look mule-stupid. The common-man from Independence, Missouri, had prevailed.

As we rode back to Oklahoma with our generator, I began to think on these things. "Sandy," I said, "Prayer Force One needs a generator like Harry Truman. Let's name it after him."

Perhaps Truman's never-say-die attitude is what America needs more of today. The Bible says that God honors the man *"that sweareth to his own hurt, and changeth not."* (Psalm 15:4) Though I don't think Harry's style of swearing was exactly what the Psalmist had in mind, I do know that Harry Truman stuck by his guns once he made a decision. Judging from his language, President Harry Truman may not have been the most reverent of Baptists, yet he had the good sense to kiss the Bible used in his presidential swearing-in ceremony, and he had the grit necessary to stay the course in the face of harsh criticism. So, if I may take the liberty of cleaning up Harry's vernacular a little, maybe we would do well to take a lesson from him and "Give 'em heaven Harry!"

Ed Moore is President and Chief Columnist for Prayer Force One
www.PrayerForceOne.com

www.PrayerForceOne.com

Chapter Eight
Using The Internet For the Glory Of God

From the two previous chapters, it can be readily seen that we have made extensive use of the Internet in order to communicate and interact with the public. Yet, only a few years ago, I, like many of those in their forties, fifties and up, found the Internet intimidating. Nevertheless, I knew that this was the direction that the world of information and communication was headed. I also knew, that those who didn't adjust to the new technology would soon be left behind. (Which of course is perfectly O.K. if you're not going anywhere.)

At that time, I had already learned to use a computer because of the need to write. Personal computers with word processors had been around for some time. Just the same, getting hooked up to the World Wide Web (The Internet), and even something as simple as getting e-mail seemed very ominous to me.

This all changed when the Lord sent our ministry a wonderful Christian man by the name of Paul Stephens. We have since become fast friends, and the things he can do with a computer make experts jealous! Because of Paul, we now operate a world-class web site, and send out some of the most beautiful, interactive e-letters in the land of cyber-space. Today, I cannot imagine operating in a world without cell phones, computers or the Internet. In fact, our ministry now relies heavily on the Internet to get our message out and to communicate with our supporters.

In this short chapter, allow me to showcase our very unique web site. In the next few pages, I would like to introduce you to some of

75

the features that make our site so very different and extremely functional.

Our Home Page Is Designed To Be Your Home Page

The first thing that I wanted to do was to design a web site that could function as a home page. For those who don't know, a home page is what your computer displays when you're connected to the internet. It can be any page you choose. However, instead of being

stuck with a home page provided by your Internet provider, we've made it easy and desirable to use *Prayer Force One* as your own home page. In order to make this desirable to the Christian public, we decided that our home page would include links to a wonderful selection of the most often used web sites. All of which are available at the click of a button.

These include such sites as *Google* and *Yahoo*, some of the internet's most powerful search engines; *CBN News*, for your daily Christian news source; *Ebay*, for those who like to shop on ebay; *Amazon*, for books, CD's and DVD's; *Wikipedia*, the free on-line encyclopedia, and *ESPN*, for those who like sports. We've even linked you to *The White House* itself for keeping you up-to-date with the President and events in the Oval Office. These buttons (shown on the left) are all located at the lower left of our web site. Just click on any of the courtesy buttons, and you're there! To return to Prayer Force One, simply close the window of the link you went to.

In order to make *Prayer Force One* your personal home page, P.C. users simply need to click on the button that

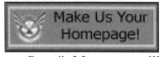

says, *"Make Prayer Force One Your Home Page"*. Mac users will have to do this manually by going to the "Preferences" option under their internet edit menu, and typing <www.PrayerForceOne.com> in the home page dialogue box.

Power Buttons

To help you in the navigation of our web site, we've also designed what we call "Power Buttons," a series of artistically enhanced buttons, that highlight some of the more interesting features of our web site.

The top button is our *"Pray In The White House"* button. As we've explained in chapter six, this is the button you would use to log into our daily virtual prayer meeting in the White House.

The second button allows you to sign up as part of *The Friends of Prayer Force One*. All information gathered from our web site is kept confidential and is used only to keep in touch with you about the Prayer Force One ministry.

The third button is your window to *a beautiful virtual tour* of our ministry flagship called Prayer Force One.

The fourth button is for those interested in reading or finding out more information about our *syndicated newspaper column*. Chapter seven covers this in detail.

The other buttons are pretty much self-explanatory ending up with the bottom button called *"Hail To The Chief."* This button contains a series of spiritual quotes made by the various presidents of the United States. Many of these quotes are also included in Part II of this book.

The Prayer Force One Times

In the middle portion of our web site, is an ever-changing electronic newspaper. Here, you will find many current news items and articles of interest about Prayer Force One. This section of our web site is always colorful, containing newsworthy photographs and other appealing graphics. Only the headlines and beginning sentences of each article are contained on the front page. To read the entire article, just click on the words *"full story"* at the bottom of any article of interest. When you're done, just close the window.

Our Monthly E-Letter

Each month, Prayer Force One sends out an e-letter to keep our friends and supporters abreast of what we are doing. This is a very

important part of our being able to stay in touch with you. To sign up for our free monthly e-letter, simply submit your e-mail address to us at the upper left corner of our web site. (pictured left) You may, of course, opt out at any time.

Forwarding Articles and E-Letters

Because Prayer Force One is a grassroots ministry, we rely on our friends to keep the word going out. One of the best and most effective ways of doing this is by forwarding our articles and e-letters to others. All of our articles and e-letters usually have a built in button that allows you to do this. Just click on the button and fill in the form with your friend's e-mail address. They will then receive the forwarded item to enjoy. Thank you for doing this often.

Other Important Buttons

There are, of course, many other important navigation buttons on our web page. The first four buttons on the left contain important information for those wanting to get acquainted with the ministry of Prayer Force One.

Immediately below these is our **"Spiritual Helps"** button for those searching for salvation or basic Bible understanding. Here you will find a selection of e-pamphlets that can be read and then forwarded to family and friends.

This area of our web site also has a place to fill out and send in a prayer request to our home office. Each week, we pray over these requests, usually aboard Prayer Force One.

The **Article Archives** contain past articles from the Prayer Force One Times. The **Column Archives** contain most of our past syndicated newspaper columns. The **E-Letter Archives** contain a vitual electronic history of Prayer Force One as preserved in our monthly e-letters. Most of these are still inter-active, just as they were originally sent out.

The last three buttons are for those who wish to make a donation to our ministry, to contact us, or who would like to make Prayer Force One their internet home page. By doing this, not only will you be able to stay abreast of the Prayer Force One ministry, but, you will be just one click away from joining our daily prayer meeting in The White House.

Finally, if you would like to link your own web site to Prayer Force One, we have

- Home
- About PF-1
- F.A.Q.'s
- Meet Our Staff
- Spiritual Helps
- Article Archives
- Column Archives
- E-Letter Archives
- Make a Donation
- Contact Us
- Make Us Your Homepage!

developed the button, (shown left) that you can download and use. To do so, just click on the button and follow directions. We also have a sister button that links your web site to our daily prayer meeting in the White House. (See page 64) You are welcome to use both.

Engraving by John C McRae, 1866

God Blesses A Praying Nation.

Chapter Nine
The Main Event:
National Prayer Force One Sunday

On Sunday, November 2, 2008 we are sponsoring and encouraging millions of Americans to participate in our first ever *National Prayer Force One Sunday*. Thereafter, this event will be held every two years on the Sunday preceding each national U. S. election.

While we have no way of knowing how many thousands or even millions may respond to this call, we do expect our prayers to move the hand of God on behalf of our nation. What exactly will occur on this day, and how can you be a part of it? This chapter is dedicated to answering these and other questions.

The first thing that everyone must realize is that we are primarily organizing *unity* in calling our nation to prayer. To do this we are also suggesting and promoting a date for this event to occur. Beyond that, our proposed *National Prayer Force One Sunday* will become what each person, what each church, and what each community decides to make of it.

Perhaps it would help to compare our *National Prayer Force One Sunday* with the way different churches and communities celebrate the Fourth of July. Just as every family, church and community celebrates the Fourth of July in their own way, and with their own events, even so, that is the way we envision this day of prayer to manifest itself. It will become whatever each individual, family, church

81

and community decides to make of it.

For example, we at Pecan Valley Baptist Church celebrate the Fourth of July by hosting an outdoor gospel concert in cooperation with our local volunteer fire department's fireworks display. The whole rural community turns out for hamburgers, hot dogs and watermelon and then we all end the evening by watching the big fireworks show. Other churches and communities may do something similar or they may do something totally different.

Likewise, this is the way I envision our *National Prayer Force One Sunday.* This event is bigger than any individual or any agenda that could possibly be prescribed. In other words, this *National Prayer Force One Sunday* should become whatever the spiritual leaders of your church or community want to make it. It may be a simple family gathering for prayer. It might be a Sunday evening service, which your particular church has dedicated and so named as part of this sacred day. It may be that the churches of your area choose to meet together in a unified evening prayer service for America. In some cases, you may want to form a committee to coordinate a much larger event. It really is up to you.

General Suggestions For You To Consider

The important thing is that we make every effort to involve as many people as possible in organizing our national appeal to heaven. Here are some suggestions on how to go about planning a *Prayer Force One Sunday* observance or event in your home, church, or community.

1. Whatever you do, do it on purpose. Make the observance one of reverence and hope. If all you do is gather your children and grandchildren around you for a special hearthside prayer service, make it special. Even as the children of Israel observed the first Passover in family settings, so I believe God will be pleased with every family prayer gathering.

2. Cottage prayer meetings are a wonderful way of gathering for this special day of prayer. Billy Graham and others have used this approach very effectively in preparing and praying for evangelistic meetings and crusades. These cottage prayer meetings can either be a one-time event on *National Prayer Force One Sunday* itself, or they may be a series of cottage prayer meetings leading up to a much

larger church or community event. The organizational aspect of this approach is especially appealing. Each cottage prayer group could be called a Prayer Force One, *Prayer Wing*, with a *Wing Leader* and *Co-Wing Leader* being in charge of coordinating the group. The value of a cottage prayer meeting should not be overlooked when considering how to lead up to a planned group effort.

3. If a larger event is desired, it is recommended that a *Prayer Force One Exploratory Committee* be formed. The job of this committee is to seek out spiritual individuals and commitments in order to set the wheels in motion for a more permanent structure which in turn can guide an effort toward a multi-church or community event. A good way to do this is to invite interested parties to a *Prayer Force One, Community Prayer Summit* in order to discuss the possibilities. Local pastors and committed lay people alike could be invited. At this meeting, important decisions could then be made and a representative group elected to guide the effort.

Suggestions For Churches To Consider

One of the greatest strengths of the kingdom of Christ on earth is the local New Testament Church. People and ideas come and go. Nations and leaders change. Customs and cultures are different. Yet, the church of Jesus Christ just keeps right on chugging along through the ages. Jesus said, *"Upon this rock I will build my church; and the gates of hell shall not prevail against it."* (Matthew 16:18)

This is why I believe that *Operation Prayer Force One* and the *National Prayer Force One Sunday* cannot succeed without major cooperation of the local New Testament churches. After all, Prayer Force One was born out of a small rural church itself. Here is a list of things that churches can do to have an effective and meaningful part on *National Prayer Force One Sunday*.

1. Make Prayer Force One a part of your church's prayer ministry. Jesus said, *"My house shall be called a house of prayer."* (Matthew 21:13) Yet, in all too many cases, prayer is the last thing that is given attention where church planning is concerned. By embracing and implementing a *National Prayer Force One Sunday* observance in your church, you will find it easier to get members focused on prayer

and to get them involved. Perhaps one Sunday night a quarter, members could be encouraged to go to go to a *Prayer Force One - Prayer Night* in the various homes of different church members. This would keep the focus on the national needs during all four seasons of the year, while providing a wonderful time of intimate fellowship between members.

2. Form a Prayer Team or Committee to coordinate the various prayer ministries of your church. This team can give special attention to coordinating the various Cottage Prayer Meetings and seeing that your church takes an active part on *National Prayer Force One Sunday*, (Sunday, Nov. 2, 2008) and the Congressionally sanctioned, *National Day of Prayer*.(The first Thursday in May each year.)

3. We encourage you to also elect or appoint an individual to serve as a *Prayer Chaplain* for your church. This individual can then act as an envoy between the church and Prayer Force One, the National Day of Prayer Task Force, The Presidential Prayer Team, etc. In this way, you will have a church liaison to interact with each of these various entities. We also have found it helpful to appoint quality individuals to serve as Prayer Captains with the church divided up into Prayer Bands or Prayer Wings. Our web site is currently developing a training course for Prayer Chaplains/Captains.

4. Download and reproduce our weekly bulletin inserts as a way of keeping a consistent prayer focus in your church. These are free to all who choose to use them and they are quite good! To use these, simply go to our web site and print off the current bulletin insert. They are designed to be copied two-up on standard 8-1/2 X 11 copy paper. When cut in half, each copy makes two bulletin inserts. The only thing that we ask is that they be used as they are, and that our web address be left on the reproduced insert.

5. If you are comfortable in doing so, consider meeting with leaders in other churches to consider sponsoring a Prayer Force One Prayer Breakfast or Prayer Rally in your community. Feel free to contact our office to request assistance in planning such an event. Our web site contains helpful suggestions for how to go about planning such an event. In limited cases, our flagship, Prayer Force One may be able to make an appearance.

National Election Dates & National Prayer Force One Sunday Dates For The Next 25 Years

*Presidential elections are identified by a "P" beside the year.

YEAR	NATIONAL PF-1 SUNDAY	ELECTION DAY
2008-P	Sunday, November 2	Tuesday, November 4
2010	Sunday, October 31	Tuesday, November 2
2012-P	Sunday, November 4	Tuesday, November 6
2014	Sunday, November 2	Tuesday, November 4
2016-P	Sunday, November 6	Tuesday, November 8
2018	Sunday, November 4	Tuesday, November 6
2020-P	Sunday, November 1	Tuesday, November 3
2022	Sunday, November 6	Tuesday, November 8
2024-P	Sunday, November 3	Tuesday, November 5
2026	Sunday, November 1	Tuesday, November 3
2028-P	Sunday, November 5	Tuesday, November 7
2030	Sunday, November 3	Tuesday, November 5
2032-P	Sunday, October 31	Tuesday, November 2

*"I still believe in America
because America still believes in God."*

Ed Moore

Chapter Ten
"In A Straight Betwixt Two."
A Brief Story Of My Life

The Bible says, "*Most men will proclaim every one his own goodness: but a faithful man who can find?*" (Proverbs 20:6) With regard to the first part of that verse, I suppose that I am no exception. However, in this brief chapter, I thought that it might be helpful to share something about my background. I do this in the hope that the reader might be able to identify their own past with the things that I have experienced and that even now motivate my life.

I entered the world in Jacksboro, Texas, on November 13, 1952, The year of my birth is inscribed on the floor of the entry hall of the White House. However, I don't think they had me in mind when they inscribed if there. Actually the year is inscribed there because this was the year when the reconstruction of the White House was completed. Truman had only recently moved back into the house. Eisenhower was president-elect by only nine days. To me at least, I like to think the date has something to do with Prayer Force One having a spiritual impact on the future of the house. To put things in perspective, this was the same year that NBC began *The Today Show*. Jackie Gleason's, *The Honeymooners*, also debuted that year, and the most popular films of the day where *Singing In The Rain*, with Gene Kelly, and *High Noon*, with Gary Cooper.

Five generations before, James Moore, Sr. had immigrated to America from Dublin, Ireland sometime before the American Revolution. His son, James Moore, Jr. moved to Tennessee where he died a short time before the Civil War. His son, my great, great,

87

grandfather, served as a 2nd Lieutenant in Company C, of the Gillispy Regiment of the Tennessee Infantry. After the war he was elected as the first County Clerk of Enders, Arkansas where he also served as its first postmaster. His grandson, my dad, moved from Arkansas to Texas, where he spent many years in the oil fields, and later, along with my mother, operated a Mom and Pop grocery store across from the county courthouse on the town square of Jacksboro, Texas.

It was here that I was born, in a small house that had been turned into a medical clinic. The same day, I was brought home to a small mobile home parked next to the *First Baptist Church* of Jacksboro. So there you have it, I was born in the wake of a presidential election and in the shadow of a church. It seems that politics and religion have competed for my attention ever since. Not until Prayer Force One came along, have I felt unity between these two contending interests. In short, most of my life has been spent *"In a straight betwixt two."* (Philippians 1:23)

My earliest years were spent in the golden wheat lands of Kay County, in north-central Oklahoma. I played in the wheat fields, rubbed wheat between my hands, and then chewed it like chewing gum many, many times. Only later in life, did I solve the mystery of why rain doesn't smell as sweet today as it did in my youth. The difference was the wheat. I grew up where, *"The waving wheat, can sure smell sweet, when the winds come right behind the rain."* (A line from our state song.) Though I have lived many places, I will always consider Blackwell, Oklahoma to be my hometown. These years were spent swimming in the Chickaskia River and sometimes ducking twisters. In Blackwell, there was a natural phobia about tornados because the town had nearly been wiped off the map by a tornado in 1955. As a boy, I can remember exploring "Clay Hills" for hidden treasures, which were really nothing more than large chunks of light green glass that had been blown all over the area when that tornado destroyed the glass plant.

In 1967, we moved to Edmond, Oklahoma, which marked a change in my life from an idyllic "Huck Finn" type of boyhood, to my Christian conversion and early manhood. Like so many today, I came from a broken home, and without much direction where religion was concerned. These were truly the turbulent sixties. However, two influences seemed to keep me from being caught up in the hippie mentality that swayed so many others of that era. The first was the lingering influence of Oklahoma's late, favorite son, Will Rogers, my boyhood hero. I even learned to spin a rope because of this remarkable man. Like Will, I was an "Okie" and proud of it. Come to think of it, with the exception of tennis shoes, (sneakers, we called them) I don't think I ever owned any kind of footwear except cowboy boots until after I was married. In fact, I even got married in a pair of cowboy boots.

The second and greatest influence of my life was my conversion to Christ at the Calvary Baptist Church of Edmond, in 1969. Will's influence gave me a natural love of humor, people and politics, while the church gave me a bedrock confidence in Christ and the Bible, which has never wavered. Even at this early age, I began to realize that my interests lay somewhere between politics and religion.

Although, I, like everyone else, was keenly conscious of President Kennedy's assassination in 1963, it was the 1968 presidential race between Richard M. Nixon and Hubert H. Humphrey that first really attracted my attention. I even acquired a little, portable, black and white television just so I could watch the two national nominating conventions. Little did I know at the time that twenty-years later, I would serve as a delegate to the 1988 Republican National Convention.

Then came Sandra Joy Corley, from the land of enchantment! Her high cheekbones and mysterious brown eyes captured my heart and have never let it go. I owe so much to her. I'm sure Billy Graham would agree that missionaries' daughters make the best wives, for he and I have both been blessed by the spiritual, levelheadedness that we have enjoyed in our "missionary-daughter" wives. When Sandy and I were married in 1973, we asked God for six children, and that is exactly what we had. (Four daughters and two sons)

College days soon followed and, like both Billy Graham, (Bob Jones College) and Ronald Reagan, (Eureka College) I went off to a small, strict, Christian college to further my education. Jack Hyles, the founder of Hyles-Anderson College in northwest Indiana, like his mentor, Bob Jones, was one of the most controversial and charismatic leaders of his day. Dr. Hyles was uncompromising and many felt that he was much too narrow. Nevertheless, this was exactly what I needed during a very volatile time of national uncertainty. Since those days, my spiritual development has also been blessed and challenged by leaders representing a broad spectrum of the Christian faith.

As always, being in a hurry about living, I managed to squeeze four years of college into three and one-half years. I worked from forty to forty-eight hours a week at Inland Steel, the largest single-location steel company in America. I worked in the labor gang of the number two open hearth furnace, making steel the old fashioned way. (Before the electric and oxygen furnaces came along.) If you've ever seen a picture of glowing-orange, molten steel being poured out of giant ladles in huge, dark, man-made caverns, this is where I toiled night after night. I believe that the hard work and long hours of those merciless days in the steel mill made me a friend forever of the working people of this nation. The men who labored among these seething hot furnaces year after unrelenting year, were a great bunch of men. I will never forget the sounds and smells, the sweat and toil, the laughter and tears, and yes, even the tragic deaths that occurred during my years at Inland Steel.

In my final days of college, I also worked at the great historic, Pullman Standard Railroad Car Company in south Chicago. This is where the legendary Pullman sleepers and dining cars were manufactured in the golden days of railroad. Little did I know that I would use many of the skills I acquired there to convert Prayer Force One into the elegant and functional dining car and sleeper that she doubles for today.

I can remember something that happened to me during college that I believe has shaped and affected my attitude and actions ever since. One day, while attending a chapel service, I felt strangely compelled to seek a personal covenant with God. At the altar that day, I said to the LORD, "*Dear God, If you will let me hear a different drumbeat, one that is distinctively from you, I promise that I will always strive to follow it, even if it is not conventional or popular.*" I felt that God both heard and accepted my offer that day, for that drumbeat has been perceptible to my spiritual ears ever since. I have always sought to follow that drumbeat, even when it seemed to make no sense at all. I believed then, and I believe now, that the cadence of that drumbeat has led me to many divine appointments, and that it will also lead me to God's ultimate destiny for my life.

As soon as I graduated from Hyles-Anderson College in the spring of 1975, Sandy and I began to raise support to go to Australia as church-planters with Baptist International Missions out of Chattanooga, Tennessee. It was during this time that we really fell in love with America as we crisscrossed its landscape. Before we were through, I would end up speaking in thirty-eight states of the Union during the American Bi-centennial Celebration. What a time to travel across the U.S.A.! We picked strawberries in Vermont, cotton in Texas, and oranges in California and Florida. We gained many friends and developed a great respect for every single state that we visited. Even though we were soon to depart from our native shores, God had placed a deep love for the whole of America in our hearts.

It was also during this time that I contracted Potomac Fever. (Which is a desire to run for public office.) In 1976, the United States experienced one of the greatest pair of presidential nominating contests in our history. On the one side, a little known, "Jimmy who?" had risen from political obscurity, to become the front-runner of the Democratic Party. On the other side, Ronald Reagan, a former movie actor and retired Governor of California, was busy sending shock waves throughout the Republican establishment by challenging the first non-elected presidential incumbent in history, Gerald R. Ford.

All of these things combined to make this one of the greatest periods of time to be traveling throughout the country. During this year, we visited the U.S. Capitol Building and the White House for the first time. We visited Williamsburg, Mount Vernon and Monticello. We walked Boston's freedom trail and visited Lexington and Concord. We spoke in Brooklyn, and saw the Statue of Liberty. I even spent a few off-days volunteering my time to the Reagan campaign during the Florida primary. *"The Spirit of '76"* had entered into our hearts and even now that year of traveling seems magical and full of wonder.

However, unbeknownst to me at the time, my heart was beginning to experience the first great battle *"betwixt"* my two developing halves.

For me, our time in Australia was one of patriotic homesickness. We became aware, for the first time, of just how deeply America was etched upon the emotions of our hearts. I found myself singing patriotic songs in the back yard of our home at 93 Manchester Road, in Gymea, New South Wales. I regularly visited the American Embassy in Sydney to read news from home, especially concerning the November election. Reagan had barely lost the nomination to Ford, and the November finale' was now being held without me. It was soon after this that I wrote the letter to Ronald Reagan to which I referred in chapter one. I found myself wanting to return home and help save my homeland from two decades of discontent and confusion. Nevertheless, Sandy and I worked hard in Australia, establishing the Southern Cross Baptist Church of Sutherland Shire, near Sydney. I'm proud to say that the church still thrives today, some thirty years later. Just the same, my heart was back in America. We soon turned the church over to a wonderful brother, by the name of Lindsey Balgowan. (Who has since gone on to heaven.) We, on the other hand, returned to Oklahoma where I had every intention of entering politics and running for the Oklahoma Legislature.

"Give a young man a chance." and *"Vote Moore for less government!"* became our campaign slogans when I first ran for the Oklahoma House of Representatives in 1978. I had two opponents in the Republican primary. Both were seasoned campaigners and one had been the Mayor of Warr Acres. When the smoke had cleared, I had garnered 49% of the vote with the other two candidates splitting the difference. However, by then, I was out of money, and my inexperience eventually brought me up short in the August runoff election. The morning after found me devastated. I was a young minister, out of work and disillusioned. I turned to carpenter work to feed my little family, as I began to pray about a very uncertain future.

In spite of my loss in the primary, I had learned some very valuable lessons. The first was that I couldn't finance a political race myself. I just didn't have the means. I came to understand, that, if I didn't believe in myself enough to raise the support of others, that I had no business running in the first place.

The second lesson was how to organize and win a campaign at the grass roots, precinct level. At a time when I was losing at large, I had tried something in one precinct, which had garnered me over 90% of the vote. It wasn't long before I knew that I had to try again. But this time, I would run for the State Senate using the lessons that I had learned in my defeat.

In 1980, I decided to run where a primary would not be an issue. I chose a seat in the Oklahoma City area that had never elected a Republican in history. In spite of a record 58 straight days of 100+ degree weather, I knocked on doors from morning till night. I wrote over 3000 handwritten letters to follow-up on those that I had visited during the day, or for that matter, to those that I had missed. Sandy and I ran what Paul Weyrich, of The Committee For The Survival Of A Free Congress, called, *"The best organized legislative campaign in America."* When the November smoke had cleared, we had won by a landslide, becoming, at age 27, the youngest State Senator ever elected in Oklahoma history. This was heady stuff!

I want to share a humorous incident that happened to me during this time that helped to keep me humble. One day, not long after I was elected, I walked onto the floor of the Senate. As I took my seat, a senate page came to me with a note stating that I had a call from the President of the United States, Ronald Reagan. I was told to take the call at the desk of the Majority Floor Leader, at the front of the Senate chamber. All kinds of things went through my head. Had the President learned of my incredible victory? Was he going to offer me some kind of position in his administration, a job so important that it warranted a call to the floor of the Senate? When I answered the phone, a ladies voice simply said, *"Senator Moore, please hold for the President."* You can imagine my embarrassment, when, after waiting for quite some time, the entire Senate stood and began clapping. I had been set up! The President had never been on the phone. All I could do was to manage a weak smile as I realized that I had just been "had" by an age-old initiation ritual of the Senate. I had not been the first, nor would I be the last. Though it smarted at the time, I have enjoyed telling about my lesson in humility many times since.

Not long after this, Morton Blackwell, a leader in the conservative movement called to offer me a job in Washington. It seems a new political action committee, called NICPAC, was being formed, This committee, which became well-known and very successful was dedicated to retiring as many liberal members of Congress as possible. Although I was honored at the offer to serve as part of its leadership, I turned the offer down, for by now, I had other plans. I had decided that if I did not make it into Congress by the time I was thirty years of age, I would go back into the ministry. My struggle *"betwixt the two"* was already entering round two.

My 1982 race for Congress against a very popular incumbent, was ill conceived from the beginning. Because my decision to run was predicated on a ridgid, self-imposed timetable, and also because the Republican Party took a beating in the 1982, off-year elections, I lost by a considerable margin. My earlier decision also made it a forgone conclusion that I would not seek re-election.

After leaving the Senate in 1984, I entered into a quiet time of raising my ever-growing family. During this time, I worked as a carpenter, building houses, or serving as a job superintendent of various construction projects. I even designed and built a 43-foot ocean going motor-sailer for missionary work in Micronesia. I also pastored a small church in south Oklahoma City, and stayed politically active within my party, eventually serving as a delegate to the 1988 Republican Presidential Nominating Convention in New Orleans, Louisiana. It was here that we heard Ronald Reagan deliver his famous, *"Give 'em one more for the Gipper!"* speech.

Although these were happy days where *"normal"* life was concerned, I have to admit that this time was somewhat like a wilderness experience where my dreams were concerned. It seemed to me that the two halves of my life were destined to clash forever, and that I had to forsake one or the other if I was ever going to find peace in either pursuit. In 1998, I accepted the pastorate of a rural Baptist Church, thirty miles east of Oklahoma City. Here, I have labored among some of the sweetest and most sincere people in the world. I determined to serve God here to the complete exclusion of any political obligations or aspirations. I was willing to serve in the obscurity of my rural pastorate for the remainder of my days, if this was what God required of me. Perhaps, I told myself, I had finally come to the place of complete surrender.

But, it was just here, at this juncture of my life, that God caught me totally off guard, and called me to the ministry of Prayer Force One. In so doing, He revealed to me the startling truth concerning the source of my conflict between politics and religion. When the light finally came on, not only did I find immediate peace and unity of heart, but I also discovered what I wholeheartedly believe to be the source of America's present dilemma as well. You see, I, like all of us in this present generation, had been taught that politics and faith must be kept separate; that coexistence was somehow illegitimate in our land of constitutional liberty. *This is the greatest folly of our time!* This ill-conceived notion has no foundation in our historical past, as I will show later. In trying to separate my patriotic and religious halves, I had been tearing my own heart in two. Frustration and confusion were the result. However, I came to understand that God did not require me to forsake one for the other. On the contrary, two halves make a whole! I suddenly realized that every bit of the confusion had been of my own making, and based on a totally false premise.

The same is true where our nation is concerned. We must come to realize that we cannot separate faith from the fabric of our nation without tearing our nation apart. (And this is exactly what is happening!) Our forefathers understood the importance of God and faith, and hence, *"In God We Trust"* was stamped on every coin lest their children should forget. (Part II of this book deals in depth with America's spiritual heritage.) During this *"great awakening"* of my understanding, I also came to realize that the orchestrated attempts of the last forty-odd years to separate the influence of faith from all things public has left America a bewildered wasteland of immorality, discontent, and confusion. (And it is taking an unforgiving toll upon our children!)

No, it is time to end this foolishness and rekindle America's spiritual heritage. Certainly, the church should not, in any official capacity, rule the nation, and vise-versa. Yet, the notion that faith in God should be divorced from all things public is foreign to hundreds of years of American history. Otherwise we could not have the words

"*In God We Trust*" on our coins or in the second verse of our national anthem. Likewise, our pledge of Allegiance could not have the words, "*under God*", nor could our congress begin each day in prayer, and so on. President Ronald Reagan stated it best when he said, "*If we ever forget that we are one nation under God, we will be a nation gone under.*" We must never let this happen!

In fact, I predict that the next great public tidal wave in America will be a re-awakening of the absolute necessity of faith in the public makeup of the nation. The success or failure of this resurgence will determine whether America fulfills her God-given destiny, or capitulates to the seduction of those deceivers who would swallow us up in the misguided objectives of the ancient failures of Babel.

Just as the two halves of my life where reunited by the discovery that religion and citizenship blend naturally in a God-given whole, so also America will only fulfill her destiny by reaffirming her faith in God. In the meantime, we must not lose heart. Although we are all tempted to look around us and dispair for our country, God is still watching over us, purging us, and preparing us. Though God-fearing Americans are tempted to become cynical and think that there is no hope for our country, we must not yield to this skepticism. We must take heart, for God has taught us time and again, that He comes to our aid when things seem the darkest. In fact, the Bible says, "*When the enemy shall come in like a flood, the Spirit of the LORD shall lift up a standard against him.*" (Isaiah 59:19)

God is not through with America, nor is He through with you. Together, and by God's grace, you and I can still turn the tide in the battle for America's soul. I believe that America's greatest days may very well lie yet before us, if we but lay our country to heart. Beloved, we are not alone in this great struggle. Never forget that there are many others who feel like you and I do; who want America to be great again. If we will close rank and do what II Chronicles 7:14 says, God will do the rest! However, there is an "*if*". The Bible says, "*If my people. . . shall humble themselves, and pray . . .*" Isn't it time that we join together and follow God's prescription for the healing of our land?

LEFT: I was born in this house in Jacksboro, Texas, on November 13, 1952. At the time it had been converted into a small town clinic. The house has since been reconverted into a home, where the birthing room is now a kitchen.

(Prayer Force One Photo)

RIGHT: My Mom and Dad, Lee and Metta Moore at the *Day & Night Grocery* which they operated in Jacksboro, Texas. Although you can't see it in this picture, the calendar reads, December 1952. My mother had given birth to me just weeks before.

LEFT: With my mother and sisters in our home town of Blackwell, Oklahoma in 1960.

RIGHT: My 1963 grade school photo at age 11.

97

LEFT: Sandra Joy Corley and I were married on June 9, 1973 in Farmington, New Mexico. She is the light and love of my life.

BELOW: This family photo was taken in 2000. God has blessed Sandy and I with two sons and four daughters.

(Photo courtesy of Blanton Photography)

RIGHT: Campaign material used in our successful 1980 race for the Oklahoma State Senate.

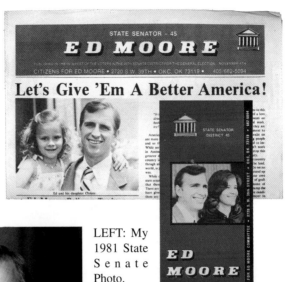

STATE SENATOR - 45

ED MOORE

PUBLISHED IN THE INTEREST OF THE VOTERS IN THE 45TH SENATE DISTRICT FOR THE GENERAL ELECTION, NOVEMBER 4TH
CITIZENS FOR ED MOORE • 2720 S.W. 39TH • OKC, OK 73119 • 405/682-5094

Let's Give 'Em A Better America!

STATE SENATOR
DISTRICT 45

ED MOORE

... PUTS YOU IN THE STATE SENATE!

LEFT: My 1981 State Senate Photo.

BOTTOM: In 1985 we designed and built *Daystar*, a 43' motor-sailer for mission use in Micronesia.

99

ABOVE: With President Ronald Reagan in the Green Room of The White House during my 1982 congressional race. (Photo courtesy of The White House)

BELOW: With Evangelist Billy Graham at the 1988 Republican National Convention in New Orleans.

ABOVE: Sandy and I at the door of Air Force One. (Sam 27000) We believe that every American should be as just as committed to the future of America as if they themselves were running for the office of President of the United States. (Photo by The Ronald Reagan Presidential Library & Museum)

BELOW: My youngest son, Tyler, and I outside the Oklahoma State Capitol in 2004. (Photo courtesy of Stephen Paul Stephens)

LEFT: Conducting a meeting in the dining car portion of *Prayer Force One*.

(Photo courtesy of Stephen Paul Stephens)

RIGHT: Looking forward at the galley area of *Prayer Force One*.

(Prayer Force One Photo)

LEFT: Looking aft at the private quarters of *Prayer Force One*.

(Prayer Force One Photo)

ABOVE: Sandy and I outside our ministry flagship, *Prayer Force One*, which is painted with the same paint as *Air Force One*. We use the similarities to emphasize the need to pray for America. The bus attracts a lot of attention wherever we go.
(Photo courtesy of Stephen Paul Stephens)

BELOW: The dining car portion of *Prayer Force One*, ready for an evening meal with supporters. The dining car seats up to twenty people. Note the lighted Washington Monument lamps on each table. (Photo courtesy of Stephen Paul Stephens)

ABOVE: Sandy and I at the Ronald Reagan Presidential Library. Our ministry is to organize and encourage Americans to pray that the LORD will give us godly leaders from the court house to the White House.   (Prayer Force One Photo)

BELOW: Our nine grandchildren represent nine good reasons why we do what we do. The tenth reason is due in March.

Part II

The Message of
Prayer Force One

*"For if the trumpet give an uncertain sound,
who shall prepare himself to the battle?"*

I Corinthians 14:8

*"If we ever forget that we're one nation under God,
then we will be a a nation gone under."*

President Ronald Reagan
August 23, 1984

Lesson One
Our National Spiritual Heritage
As Presented In Presidential Quotes

When George Washington took the oath of office as the first President of the United States, he placed his left hand upon the Bible. He did not do this because it was required by the Constitution, but because it was the natural and right thing to do in America. When he finished taking the presidential oath, he added the words, "*So help me God*." Again, this was not required. Then, in somber reverence, and in the sight of all of those present, the nation's first president bent and kissed the Bible that had been used during the ceremony. This first official act of a United States President says it all. This was a nation that owed its existence to God Almighty. Every single president, since George Washington, has also taken the presidential oath upon the Bible. Likewise, every single one of them has added the words, "*So help me God*." This is our spiritual heritage!

Yet, sadly, this is also a heritage that we are quickly forgetting. Indeed, in the last fifty years, there has been an orchestrated effort to deny and destroy the validity of this spiritual heritage. Unfortunately, many today are buying into this great deception. However, to anyone who knows anything about the spiritual history of this country, one thing becomes perfectly clear: freedom *of* religion was never meant to mean freedom *from* religion in all things public. Yet, this is the perverted concept that the perpetrators of this philosophy would have us to believe. The result is that we are moving toward a society in which God, religion, and faith are not publicly welcome. Even now, in many cases, government itself has become hostile toward religion. We are told that our children cannot pray in public schools as they did for over one

107

hundred and fifty years. We are also being told that public prayers cannot be offered *"in Jesus' name,"* and that military chaplains must minister to some *"generic god."* In the mean time, every sort of vile wickedness is given *"Constitutional protection"* while the church is treated like some threatening plague. In short, what evil, godless communism could not force upon the Russian people in a hundred years, this wicked philosophy has nearly accomplished in America in half the time! The Bible warns,

> *"Woe unto them that call evil good, and good evil;*
> *that put darkness for light, and light for darkness;*
> *that put bitter for sweet, and sweet for bitter. . . because*
> *they have cast away the law of the LORD of hosts."*
>
> (Isaiah 5:20,24)

In order to check and reverse the encroachment of this hateful, humanistic, anti-God philosophy, we must go back and rediscover what our forefathers actually said and practiced in a *public* context. In doing this, it will become very evident that what made America great were her spiritual foundations. Although there are many appropriate quotes from every sector of public life throughout our history, we need only to confine ourselves to the utterances of our presidents in order to see that the foundations of our republic were founded upon God, the Bible, and Christianity.

George Washington
First President of the United States

As we have seen, George Washington set some very strong and undeniable spiritual precedents while taking the oath of office. However, he also made some very clear and unmistakable declarations where God and our nation were concerned. In his First Inaugural Address, President Washington stated:

> *"It would be peculiarly improper to omit in this first*
> *official act, my fervent supplications to that Almighty*
> *Being, who rules over the universe, who presides in the*
> *councils of nations, and whose providential aids can*

supply every human defect, that His benediction may
consecrate to the liberties and happiness of the people
of the United States, a government instituted by
themselves for these essential purposes. . . "

Here it is easy to see, that Washington wanted it to be clearly understood that his first official act as president was to pray for Divine blessings upon the nation. President Washington went on to state the reason that such prayer was both appropriate and necessary. He said:

"No people can be bound to acknowledge and
adore the Invisible Hand which conducts the affairs
of men more than those of the United States. Every
step by which they have advanced to the character of
an independent nation, seems to have been
distinguished by some token of Providential agency."

Washington went on to invoke, *"pious gratitude,"* and a *"humble anticipation of future blessings."* He then makes the following declaration, a declaration that we, as Americans, need to hear again today. We quote:

"The propitious smiles of Heaven can never be
expected on a nation that disregards the eternal rules of
order and right, which Heaven itself has ordained."

When one considers both the tone and content of President Washington's *First Inaugural Address*, it would not be extreme to call it his *"First Inaugural Sermon"*. Again, it was George Washington, who instituted our first national Thanksgiving, to be observed on November 26, 1789. His final *Farewell Address* was also full of reverence and prayer for Divine blessings. In it, he stated:

"Reason and experience both forbid us to expect
that national morality can exist apart from religious
principle."

How we desperately need to realize this again today. A final quote from George Washington underscores the widespread founding sentiments of our newly formed nation. He firmly stated:

"It is impossible to rightly govern the world without
God and the Bible!"

To this, we say, Amen!

John Adams
Second President of the United States

 As a historian, it is hard for me to imagine the United States without the Adams family. If George Washington was, *"The Father of Our Country,"* then most certainly, Samuel Adams was, *"The Father of the American Revolution,"* for it was he and his *"Sons of Liberty"* who set the revolutionary ball in motion. However, what Sam Adams was to America's independence movement, his cousin, John Adams, our second president, was to the Continental Congress. John Adams served on 23 of the 26 committees appointed by that body, including the committee to draft the Declaration of Independence. If anyone understood the role that faith should play in American public life, it would be John Adams. In fact, John Adams boldly stated:

"I consider a decent respect for Christianity among the best recommendations for public service."

It was also John Adams who wrote, what has probably become the most famous prayer ever offered in American history. In fact this prayer is the very first recorded act, performed by any president in the White House. On his first night in the nearly completed Executive Mansion, John Adams, pen in hand, wrote the words of this prayer to his dear wife, Abigail:

"I pray Heaven to bestow the best of blessings on this house and all that shall hereafter inhabit it. May none but honest and wise men ever rule under this roof."

I like to imagine the night on which John Adams prayed this prayer. I think I see the new house cradled by the chilly blue of that early November evening. I picture the President in his evening robe, sitting by one of the first fires to blaze within a White House hearth. I imagine this prayer slowly and reverently winding its way upward toward heaven, and entering into the eternal ears of God. I believe that prayer still echoes in the halls of heaven today. Nearly 130 years after John Adams penned this prayer, President Franklin Delano

Roosevelt would have the words of this immortal prayer carved on the mantle of the State Dining Room of the White House. These words remain there today for every White House visitor to see.

Thomas Jefferson
Third President of the United States

President Thomas Jefferson is probably one of the most misrepresented of all the presidents, where his spiritual views are concerned. The letter that he wrote to a friend, in which he refers to an invisible wall of separation between church and state, has been completely and utterly misrepresented, as we will show in lesson five. Jefferson's spiritual views, where appropriate public expression is concerned, are  clearly demonstrated in this, his *Presidential Prayer For Peace*, dated March 4, 1805.

> *"Almighty God, who has given us this good land for our heritage: We humbly beseech Thee that we may always prove ourselves a people mindful of Thy favor and glad to do Thy will. Bless our land with honorable ministry, sound learning, and pure manners. Save us from violence, discord, and confusion, from pride and arrogance and from every evil way. Defend our liberties, and fashion into one united people the multitude brought hither out of many kindreds and tongues. Endow with Thy spirit wisdom those whom in Thy Name we entrust the authority of government, that there may be justice and peace at home, and that through obedience to Thy law, we may show forth Thy praise among the nations of earth. In time of prosperity fill our hearts with thankfulness, and in the day of trouble, suffer not our trust in Thee to fail; all of which we ask through Jesus Christ our Lord. Amen."*

This is not quite the Thomas Jefferson that we have been led to believe existed, is it? Yet, this is the man who penned our Declaration of Independence, *in which*, we, as a nation, acknowledged God as Creator. Those who would rob us of our spiritual heritage, not only deny God's creative authority, but would replace it with a view of unprovable evolutionary blasphemy taught as science, falsely so called. (I Timothy 6:20-21) No thank you, we prefer the acknowledgement of God as Creator, just as President Thomas Jefferson did.

President James Madison
Fourth President of the United States

James Madison, at five foot, four inches and only one hundred pounds, was the smallest of all our presidents. Yet Madison was a giant intellectually. Known as *"The Father of the Constitution,"* James Madison's contribution to *The Federalist Papers* give us one of our most powerful looks into the minds of those who forged the Constitution. The following statement by President Madison serves not only as a monument to the faith of our founding fathers, but also clearly acknowledges God's law as the very foundation of our Constitution.

"We have staked the whole future of American civilization not on the power of government, far from it. We have staked the whole of our political institutions upon the capacity of mankind for self-government, upon the capacity of each and all of us to govern ourselves according to the commandments of God. The future and success of America is not in this Constitution, but in the laws of God upon which this Constitution is founded."

Isn't it incredible that the *"Father of the Constitution"* acknowledged the commandments of God as the undergirdings of our Constitution, while modern judges tell us that we cannot even have the Ten Commandments in our government buildings, let alone in our public schools? Isn't it appalling how far these misguided judges have departed from the truth? We must rally before it is too late!

John Quincy Adams
Sixth President of the United States

John Quincy Adams, the son of John Adams, was the only son of a former president to also serve as president. That is, until the election of George W. Bush in 2000. John Quincy Adams was a devout Christian who spoke for an entire generation of Americans when he connected Christianity with the foundations of the new government. Notice what he said:

> *"The Highest glory of the American Revolution was this; that it connected in one indissoluble bond, the principles of self-government with the principles of Christianity."*

Andrew Jackson
Seventh President of the United States

Old Hickory was not a man to mince words, nor lose battles. Andrew Jackson became famous for his victory over the British at the Battle of New Orleans, losing only thirteen men while the British lost over 2000. Andrew Jackson knew that his victories were of God.

In both of his inaugural addresses, Jackson publicly acknowledged his reliance upon God. In the second address he said:

> *"Finally, it is my most fervent prayer to that Almighty Being before whom I now stand, and who has kept us in His hands from the infancy of our Republic unto the present day, that He will so overrule all my intentions and actions and inspire the hearts of my fellow-citizens that we may be preserved from dangers of all kinds and continue forever a united and happy people."*

President Jackson's most powerful and oft repeated quote

concerning our nation and its reliance upon the Bible is this.

"The Bible is the rock upon which this Republic rests!"

Isn't it about time that we quit allowing the foundations of our Republic to be discarded? Yea, isn't it about time for us to repair these foundations?

Abraham Lincoln
Sixteenth President of the United States

Abraham Lincoln once said of the Bible, *"I believe the Bible is the best gift God ever gave to man. All the good from the Savior of the world is communicated to us through that book."* On a personal spiritual note, Lincoln confessed, *"I have been driven many times to my knees with the overwhelming conviction, that I had nowhere else to go."*

President Lincoln was not only deeply religious in his personal life, but also believed in the vital importance of religion and faith as the foundation of all good government. Notice how Abraham Lincoln used the word *"duty"* in referring to a nation's spiritual obligation to acknowledge God.

"It is the duty of nations as well as men, to own
their dependence upon the overruling power of God
and to recognize the sublime truth announced in the
Holy Scriptures and proven by all history, that those
nations only are blessed whose God is the LORD."

Lincoln also defended the United States courts of his day for basing moral decisions on Biblical standards, which the courts had consistently done for over half a century. In this regard he stated:

"The only assurance of our nation's safety is to lay
our foundation in morality and religion."

President Lincoln was sincere in this conviction. I do not think that it is unfair to say that the end of slavery and the preservation of the Union might never had occurred had it not been for the Bible-based convictions which fortified and compelled Lincoln both before and during his presidency.

Theodore Roosevelt
Twenty-sixth President of the United States

President Theodore Roosevelt was undoubtedly one of our nation's greatest presidents. Like his personal hero, Abraham Lincoln, T.R. was also a man of deep personal faith. Again, like Lincoln, he literally changed the world in which he lived. He did so because of his strong belief that right was clearly set forth in the Bible. This attitude can easily be seen in the following quote in which Theodore

Roosevelt warned the nation that the Bible must remain as the foundation of our national morality.

> *"Every thinking man, when he thinks, realizes that the teachings of the Bible are so interwoven and intertwined with our whole civic and social life that it would be literally, I do not mean figuratively, but literally impossible for us to figure what the loss would be if these teachings were removed. We would lose all the standards by which we now judge both public and private morals; all the standards toward which we, with more or less resolution, strive to raise ourselves."*

Unfortunately, our generation is now seeing the result of a generation where Biblical morality has been nationally purged.

Woodrow Wilson
Twenty-eighth President of the United States

President Woodrow Wilson was the son of a Presbyterian minister. During his remarkable life he was a historian, lecturer, educator, President of Princeton University, Governor of New Jersey and President of the United States. If any man was in a position to know the truth about America's spiritual and political credentials, it was Woodrow Wilson. Two years before taking office as President of the United

States, Woodrow Wilson boldly declared the truth about America's birth and then followed it with a personal challenge to everyone present. He said:

"America was born a Christian nation. America was born to exemplify that devotion to the elements of righteousness, which are derived from Holy Scripture. Ladies and gentlemen, I have a very simple thing to ask of you. I ask of every man and woman in this audience that, from this night on, they will realize that part of the destiny of America lies in their daily perusal of this great Book of revelations. (The Bible) That if they would see America free and pure they will make their own spirits free and pure by the baptism of Holy Scripture."

Calvin Coolidge
Thirtieth President of the United States

Calvin Coolidge was a man of few words. Known as *"Silent Cal"* he often said that he could carry on whole conversations by only using two words, *yes* and *no*. A lady once told President Coolidge that she had bet she could make the President say more than two words. To which he dryly replied, *"You lose."* Therefore, being a man of few words, perhaps we should put greater weight on the words that he did speak, especially concerning America's foundations. He said:

"The foundations of our society and our government rest so much on the teachings of the Bible, that it would be difficult to support them if faith in these teachings would cease to be practically universal in our country."

In the following statements, President Coolidge is quite clear:

"If American democracy is to remain the greatest hope of humanity, it must continue abundantly in the faith of the Bible"   (May 3, 1925)

*"No ambition, no temptations, lures her thought
to foreign dominations. The legions, which she sends
forth, are armed, not with sword, but with the Cross.
The higher state to which she seeks the allegiance of
all mankind is not of human, but of Divine origin. She
cherishes no purpose save to merit the favor of
Almighty God."* (Inaugural Address, March 4, 1925)

Herbert Hoover
Thirty-first President of the United States

Although Ronald Reagan is said to have
patterned his presidential *"style"* after that of
Franklin Roosevelt, Reagan openly praised the
presidencies of Calvin Coolidge and Herbert
Hoover. In praising the latter, Reagan showed
remarkable courage inasmuch as Hoover had
become the national whipping-boy for the great
depression. However, before the stock market
crash of '29, Hoover was universally acclaimed
and respected. Today, history is beginning to display a fairer view of
this remarkable man and his ill-fated presidency.

Actually, Hoover understood that real recovery had to come from
character within more than from anything government programs could
do. Hoover wrote:

*"Our social and economic system cannot march
toward better days unless it is inspired by things of
the Spirit. It is here that the higher purposes of
individualism must find their sustenance."*

Those, who only look to government for solutions, cannot
comprehend what Hoover meant. But, those who do not barter the
welfare of their nation's children for immediate financial expediency,
understand exactly what he meant. Herbert Hoover's sentiments
toward the dangers of excessive indulgence have now proven to be
prophetic. Concerning America's strengths and challenges he wrote:

*"Our strength lies in spiritual concepts. It lies in
public sensitivities to evil. Our greatest danger is not*

from invading armies. Our dangers are that we may
commit suicide from within by complaisance with evil,
or by public tolerance of scandalous behavior."

Does not this warning ring eerily true in the face of today's immolations to cinematic sin?

Franklin Delano Roosevelt
Thirty-second President of the United States

On June 6, 1944, President Franklin Roosevelt went on national radio with these solemn words:

"My fellow Americans: Last night when I spoke with you about the fall of Rome, I knew at that moment that the troops of the United States and our allies were crossing the channel in another and greater operation. It has come to pass with success thus far. And so, in this poignant hour, I ask you to join me in prayer:

Almighty God: Our sons, pride of our nation, this day have set upon a mighty endeavor, a struggle to preserve our Republic, our religion, and our civilization. . ."

Take personal note that President Roosevelt specifically invoked God's blessings in order to protect, among other things, *our religion.* How can it be that it is constitutional for our President to pray; for our Congress to start each day in prayer; for our courts to begin each session in prayer, and yet, that it is somehow unconstitutional for our children to do the same? On October 28, 1944, Roosevelt expressed his deep conviction about the value of Christianity to democracy.

"'Peace on earth, good will toward men' - democracy must cling to that message. For it is my deep conviction that democracy cannot live without that true religion which gives a nation a sense of justice and moral purpose."

The only man to be elected president for four consecutive terms could not have put it any more eloquently than this.

Harry S. Truman
Thirty-third President of the United States

Harry S. Truman was probably the most unlikely of all of our U.S. presidents. He had failed in three businesses. At the age of 50, no one in Washington had ever heard of him. Yet, Harry Truman assumed the presidency at one of the most critical times in American history. In his first address to Congress after the death of Roosevelt he spoke these words:

> *" At this moment, I have in my heart a prayer. As I have assumed my heavy duties, I humbly pray, Almighty God, in the words of King Solomon: 'Give therefore thy servant an understanding heart to judge thy people, that I may discern between good and bad, for who is able to judge this thy so great people?' I ask only to be a good and faithful servant of my LORD and my people."*

Harry Truman was a common man with uncommon sense. He was as American as apple pie. Truman was underestimated when he took office and only now is history beginning to realize the true greatness of the man and his presidency. Concerning the origins of our fundamental American rights, Truman had this to say:

> *"The basis of our Bill of Rights comes from the teachings we get from Exodus and St. Matthew, from Isaiah and St. Paul. I don't think we emphasize that enough these days. If we don't have a proper fundamental moral background, we will finally end up with a government which does not believe in rights for anybody but the state!"*

Harry Truman firmly believed in the faith-based foundations of our Constitution. In the following statement, Truman underscored his faith in God as Creator and as the author of human equality. Speaking on behalf of our American beliefs, he said:

> *"We believe that all men are created equal because we were created in the image of God."*

Dwight D. Eisenhower
Thirty-fourth President of the United States

Few presidents have enjoyed such universal public esteem as President Dwight D. Eisenhower. He had been the victorious Supreme Commander of all allied forces during WWII. He then presided over an era of unprecedented growth and prosperity. In a world, then threatened by the godless atheism of world communism, Eisenhower countered:

"Without God, there could be no American form of government, nor an American way of life. Recognition of the Supreme Being is the first, the most basic expression of Americanism."

Lyndon Baines Johnson
Thirty-sixth President of the United States

Lyndon Baines Johnson once asked Evangelist Billy Graham to run for President of the United States. And why not, hadn't President James A. Garfield been a minister of the gospel of Jesus Christ? Remember, Billy Graham was just over fifty years of age and at the height of his popularity. This did not seem strange to Lyndon Johnson, who himself was the great-grandson of one of the most respected Baptist ministers in Texas. While he was President, Johnson liked to show people a letter from Sam Houston to his great-grandfather, Reverend George Washingtion Baines. Sr. He always told the story of how his great grandfather had led Sam Houston to faith in Christ. It would be interesting to consider how history might have been different if Billy Graham had been elected President in 1968 instead of Richard Nixon.

On February 1, 1961, Vice-President Johnson said:

"We need to remember that the separation of church and state must never mean the separation of religious values from the lives of public servants. . . If we who

*serve free men today are to differ from the tyrants of
this age, we must balance the powers in our hands
with God in our hearts."*

James Earl Carter, Jr.
Thirty-ninth President of the United States

President Carter has earned enduring
respect on three fronts. First, for obtaining the
Presidency against seemingly impossible odds.
Second, for brokering a lasting peace between
Egypt and Israel; and third, for his continued
influence for peace after leaving office. He
remains one of only three American presidents
to win a Nobel Peace Prize. Carter's *"born
again"* rhetoric during the 1976 presidential
campaign caused some, in certain quarters, to question whether one
so apparently committed to his Christian faith could govern
effectively. President Carter responded to this by stating:

*"You can't divorce religious belief and public
service. . . I've never detected any conflict between
God's will and my political duty. If you violate one,
you violate the other."*

Today, few deny that President Carter's firmly held Christian
beliefs led to his well-deserved legacy as an international peacemaker.

Ronald Wilson Reagan
Fortieth President of the United States

I counted it a great personal honor to
have visited with President Reagan in the
White House in 1982. From the beginning,
it was clear to me that Ronald Reagan fully
comprehended the need for national spiritual
renewal. As you would expect from *"The
Great Communicator,"* he left us a wealth of
quotes that beautifully articulate the role
of faith as part of our national fabric. The

difficulty for me, in writing this section, has not been in finding good quotes, but in selecting the quotes which best exemplify his views on God and faith as it relates to the welfare of our nation. I finally decided to include most of these quotes here and then add others in later lessons, where they seem to be the most appropriate. My favorite quote is a comment President Reagan made in a speech in Dallas, on August 23, 1984. He said:

> *"Without God, there is no virtue, because there's no prompting of the conscience. Without God, we're mired in the material, that flat world that tells us only what our senses perceive. Without God, there is a coarsening of the society. And without God, democracy will not and cannot long endure. If we ever forget that we're one nation under God, then we will be a nation gone under."*

The last sentence of the above quote should be put on billboards all across the United States, so that every adult citizen, every teenager and yes, every child in America could be reminded of this great truth.

Reagan based his philosophy, like those of the presidents who preceded him, upon the expressed belief in God as Creator. On September 21, in a nationally televised presidential debate, and just weeks before his landslide victory, Reagan said:

> *"Going around this country, I have found a great hunger in America for spiritual revival; for a belief that law must be based on a higher law; for a return to traditions and values that we once had. Our government, in its most sacred documents - the Constitution and the Declaration of Independence and all - speak of man being created, of a Creator; that we're a nation under God."*

Likewise, in his National Day of Prayer Proclamation, dated January 29, 1985, President Reagan spoke of the *"appropriateness"* of national prayer. He said:

> *"We are all God's handiwork, and it is appropriate for us as individuals and as a nation to call on Him in prayer."*

President Ronald Reagan not only believed that we should pray as a nation, but he sincerely believed that there could be no liberty without the blessings of God. On March 8, 1983, Reagan said:

"Freedom prospers only where the blessings of God are avidly sought, and humbly accepted."

This progression of thought from Ronald Reagan's mind flowed naturally because he, being the oldest elected president, literally sprang from an era that was still in-sync with the America that was, and had always been. He is one of those vocal few that both saw and warned against the encroachment of government in seeking to redefine America's spiritual past, especially by the courts. Listen to his words dated, February 4, 1982:

"Sometimes it seems we've strayed . . . from our convictions that standards of right and wrong do exist and must be lived up to. God, the source of our knowledge, has been expelled from the classroom. He gives us His greatest blessing, life, and yet many would condone the taking of innocent life. We expect Him to protect us in crisis, but turn away from Him too often in our day-to-day living. I wonder if He isn't waiting for us to wake up."

However, where Reagan was concerned, he was already awake, and stated his spiritual goals for the nation in his *"Goals for the Future"* radio address, given from Camp David on August 25, 1984.

"Our goal is to help revive America's traditional values; faith, family, neighborhood, work, and freedom. Government has no business enforcing these values, but neither must it seek, as it did in the recent past, to suppress or replace them. That only robbed us of our tiller, and set us adrift.

Helping to restore these values will bring new strength, direction, and dignity to our lives and to the life of our nation. It is on these values that we'll best build our future."

My prayer is that we will return to the wisdom expressed in these lofty goals, set forth by President Ronald Reagan.

George H. W. Bush
Forty-first President of the United States

George Herbert Walker Bush, like George Washington, seems to have been Providentially rescued from the arms of certain death. During the French and Indian War, George Washington had several horses shot out from under him and bullets penetrated his coat many times. Likewise, George Bush received the Distinguished Flying Cross after flying fifty-eight missions and being shot down in the Pacific during World War II. At his inaugurated, George Bush said:

"My first act as President is a prayer. I ask you to bow your heads: Heavenly Father, we bow our heads and thank You for Your love. Accept our thanks for the peace that yields this day and the shared faith that makes its continuance likely. Make us strong to do Your work, willing to heed and hear Your will, and write on our hearts these words: 'Use power to help people.' For we know that we are given power, not to advance our own purposes, nor to make a great show in the world, nor a name. There is but one just use of power, and it is to serve people. Help us to remember it Lord. Amen."

Largely as a result of the policies, which the Reagan-Bush administrations set into motion, America witnessed the end of the cold war, the destruction of the Berlin Wall, and the collapse of the Soviet Union. Concerning this, President Bush plainly gave God the credit by stating:

"We asked for God's help; and now, in this shining outcome, in this magnificent triumph of good over evil, we should thank God."

It is also interesting to note that it was George Bush who dedicated the presidential *Evergreen Chapel*, which was constructed at Camp David during the Reagan-Bush administration. (See lesson four to learn more about this.)

George W. Bush
Forty-third President of the United States

The presidency of George W. Bush has faced challenges that dwarf all but a limited number of those faced by other presidents. It appears that George Bush sensed this long before he ever became his party's nominee. On a nationally televised religious program sponsored by Evangelist James Robinson, presidential candidate George Bush said:

> *"I feel like God wants me to run for president. I can't explain it, but I sense my country is going to need me. Something is going to happen. I know it won't be easy on my family, but God wants me to do it."*

Today, in light of all that has transpired since 9/11, these words now seem prophetic. George Bush, has, from the beginning, been very candid and unapologetic about his personal faith in Jesus Christ. For President Bush, his actions are a natural outflow of the inner workings of his faith. Explaining this he said:

> *"Faith is the framework for living. It gives us the spirit and heart that affects everything we do. If gives us hope each day. Faith gives us purpose to right wrongs, to preserve our families, and to teach our children values. Faith gives us conscience to keep us honest, even when nobody is looking. And, faith can change lives; I know first hand, because faith changed mine."*

President Bush went on to describe how this personal life changing faith in Christ also affects his job as President.

> *"My relationship with God through Christ has given me meaning and direction. My faith has made a big difference in my personal life, and my public life as well. I make personal decisions every day. Some are easy, and some aren't so easy. I have worries just like you do. And I pray. I pray for guidance. I pray for*

> *patience. I firmly believe in the power of intercessory*
> *prayer; and I know that I could not do my job without*
> *it."*

President Bush, correctly and unmistakably links liberty and the founding documents of our nation to the Creator of life. He said:

> *"America stands for liberty, for the pursuit of*
> *happiness and for the inalienable right to life. This*
> *right to life cannot be granted nor denied by*
> *government, because it does not come from*
> *government, it comes from the Creator of life."*

The Obvious Conclusion

I apologize for not being able to quote every single president. My goal has been to present representative selections of presidential quotes from all parties and from all periods of American history. In weighing the overwhelming evidence of our national spiritual heritage, as represented by this compendium of presidential quotes, it must be concluded that our national heritage is based upon Christianity, the Bible and upon our national faith in God. To deny this is to deny the weighty evidence that our presidents and others have so richly endowed us.

While our Constitution guarantees the right to worship as one pleases, it does not ban religion from being part of our public, legislative or judicial life. On the contrary, our long history and the public expressions of our presidents clearly prove otherwise. This is why every single president of the United States took the oath of office upon the Holy Bible.

I believe that the heritage presented here should be taught to our children in public schools, not to establish *"a religion"*, but because these things are historical fact. When and if such lessons also become unconstitutional; when we can no longer even quote the utterances of our nation's presidents because they contain references to God and the Bible, then we will have truly renounced the faith of our fathers and become the unworthy heirs of the spiritual heritage they left to us. In the meantime, let us teach our children what our nation's presidents have said. And why not? After all, it's our American heritage!

Lesson One: Open Book Quiz
(See how much you can remember. The answers are on page 243)

1. What words did George Washington add to the end of the presidential oath of office? _____

2. What is the first recorded act of any president in The White House, and by which president? _____ by _____

3. What book has every U.S. President laid his hand on, while taking the presidential oath of office? _____

4. How many presidents have repeated the words, "*So help me God*" during the swearing in ceremony? _____

5. According to President James Madison, what is the U.S. Constitution founded upon? _____

6. According to John Quincy Adams, what two sets of principles where bonded together by the American Revolution? _____ _____ and _____

7. Fill in the blanks of this statement by President Andrew Jackson. "*The _____ is the _____ upon which this Republic rests!*"

8. Fill in the blanks of this statement by President Abraham Lincoln. "*It is the _____ of _____ as well as men, to own their dependence upon the overruling power of _____.*"

9. Abraham Lincoln said, "*Those nations only are blessed whose God is _____ _____.*"

10. Which president said, "*America was born a Christian nation.*"? _____.

11. Complete this statement by President Calvin Coolidge. "*If American democracy is to remain the greatest _____ of humanity, it must continue abundantly in the _____ of the _____.*"

12. Complete this statement by President Dwight Eisenhower. "*Without _____, there could be no American form of government, nor an American way of life. Recognition of the _____ _____ is the first, the most basic expression of Americanism.*"

13. Which president said, "*If we ever forget that we're one nation under God, then we will be a nation gone under.*"? _____

14. Which president said, "*My first act as President is a prayer.*"? _____

The Constitutional Convention
Philidelphia, 1787

Lesson Two

Our Nation's Founding Fathers

The Evidence Of Our Nation's Founders and Early Educators

America Was Founded As A Christian Nation

While our Founding Fathers were careful to safeguard individual freedom of worship, (a virtue extended almost exclusively in Christian nations) they had no intention of disenfranchising the Christian faith or undermining its influence upon the civil and moral laws of the nation. Our founders readily acknowledged that this nation was founded as a Christian nation and upon the principles of the Bible. Evidence abounds in this regard. In this lesson, we will explore the testimony of other patriots from America's founding period. In addition to the quotes of our Presidents, and as a transition, to tie this lesson with the previous one, allow me to again quote President John Quincy Adams, who said:

> *"The birthday of this nation is indissolubly linked with the birthday of the Savior, [and] forms a leading event in the progress of the gospel dispensation. . . The Declaration of Independence. . . laid the cornerstone of human governments upon the first precepts of Christianity."*

President Woodrow Wilson was plainer yet when he said:

> *"America was born a Christian nation. America was born to exemplify that devotion to the elements of righteousness, which are derived from Holy Scripture."*

However, in addition to what our presidents have said, there are many other early Americans who bore witness to this great truth.

John Jay,
Our First Supreme Court Justice

Because our current problems are traceable to illicit rulings of recent past courts, especially the Supreme Court, allow me to begin with John Jay, the first *Chief Justice of the United States Supreme Court*. Prior to this honor, John Jay served as *President of The Second Continental Congress*. He, along with James Madison and Alexander Hamilton, co-wrote *The Federalist Papers* in a tireless effort to get the Constitution ratified. Jay later served two terms as the *Governor of New York* and also as *President of the American Bible Society*. In other words, John Jay was endowed with some of the greatest credentials of any of the Founding Fathers. So, what did our first Chief Justice say about Christianity and politics? I quote:

> *"Providence has given our people the choice of their rulers, and it is the duty as well as the privilege and interest of our Christian nation to select and prefer Christians for their rulers."*

Kindly take note that our first Supreme Court justice considered it the *"duty"* of *"our Christian nation"* to *"select and prefer Christians for their rulers."* It would seem that our recent high court justices would do well to re-read the opinion of our Supreme Court's Founding Father.

Patrick Henry,
Firebrand of the Revolution

Few patriots so inflamed the cause of the American Revolution as Patrick Henry. What Sam Adams and James Otis were to Massachusetts and the northern colonies, Patrick Henry and George Mason were to Virginia and the southern colonies. Patrick Henry was not only the Commander-in-Chief of the Virginia Militia, but served as a delegate to the Continental Congress. Although Henry was instrumental in pressing for the passage of The Bill of Rights, it is his famous speech in St. John's Church, in Richmond, Virginia, that he is most fondly remembered today. He concluded his fiery speech with these powerful and haunting words:

> *"Is life so dear, or peace so sweet, as to be purchased at the price of chains and slavery? Forbid it Almighty God! I know not what course others may take; but as for me, give me liberty or give me death."*

Indeed, Patrick Henry was so popular during his life that he was elected as Governor of Virginia for six consecutive terms, and turned down offers by Washington to be the first Secretary of State or first Chief Justice of the Supreme Court! Here is what Patrick Henry had to say about the foundation of the United States.

> *"It cannot be emphasized too strongly or too often that this great nation was founded, not by religionists, but by Christians; not on religions, but on the Gospel of Jesus Christ! For this very reason, peoples of other faiths have been afforded asylum, prosperity, and freedom of worship here."*

How desperately America needs to be reminded again that America is great because were founded as a Christian nation!

George Mason, Father of the Bill of Rights

One cannot possibly overlook George Mason when considering the Founding Fathers. Just a year before his death, Thomas Jefferson said of Mason:

> *"The fact is unquestionable, that the Bill of Rights, and the Constitution of Virginia, were drawn originally by George Mason, one of our really great men, and of the first order of greatness."*

President Harry Truman summed up Mason's under-appreciated greatness and influence saying:

> *"Too few Americans realize the vast debt we owe*

*to George Mason. His immortal Declaration of Rights
in 1776 was one of the finest and loftiest creations
ever struck from the mind of man. George Mason it
was who first gave concrete expression to those
inalienable human rights that belong to every
American citizen and that today are the bedrock of
our democracy. Our matchless Bill of Rights came
directly from the amazing wisdom and far-seeing
vision of this patriot."*

So what did George Mason, the Father of our Bill of Rights, have
to say about God and government? Consider this awesome statement.

*"As nations cannot be rewarded or punished in
the next world they must be in this. By an inevitable
chain of causes and effects, Providence punishes
national sins, by national calamities."*

This truth should bear great weight upon our national conscience.

Benjamin Franklin,
Sage of the Constitutional Convention

With the possible exception of George
Washington, none of our Founding Fathers was
more venerated than Benjamin Franklin. It is
not stretching the truth to say, that although
Franklin was too old to fight in the American
Revolution, humanly speaking, he was
probably more responsible for winning the war
than any other American. Had it not been for
Franklin's brilliant diplomatic prowess in
securing the French alliance, the disposition of the war almost certainly
would have turned out very differently.

Later, during the Constitutional Convention of 1787, Benjamin
Franklin once again stepped up to the plate and hit a home run. By all
accounts, the convention had stalemated over complicated
constitutional issues. Differences of opinions and heated emotions
were causing deep division and discord. Hostility was rapidly forming
between the larger and smaller states. Just as the Convention was

reaching the boiling point, 81 year-old Benjamin Franklin stood and turned the tide with a wise and powerful speech. James Madison recorded his words, an excerpt of which is included here. Addressing George Washington, the President of the convention, Franklin said:

> *"In this situation of this assembly, groping as it were in the dark to find political truth, and scarce able to distinguish it when presented to us, how has it happened, Sir, that we have not hitherto once thought of humbly applying to the Father of lights to illuminate our understanding? In the beginning of the contest with Great Britain, when we were sensible of danger, we had daily prayer in this room for Divine protection. Our prayers, Sir, were heard and graciously answered. All of us who were engaged in the struggle must have observed frequent instances of a superintending Providence in our favor. To that kind Providence, we owe this happy opportunity of consulting in peace on the means of establishing our future national felicity. And have we now forgotten that powerful Friend? Or do we imagine that we no longer need His assistance?*
>
> *I have lived Sir, a long time, and the longer I live, the more convincing proofs I see of this great truth - 'That God governs in the affairs of men.' And if a sparrow cannot fall to the ground without His notice, is it probable that an empire can rise without His aid? We have been assured, Sir, in the sacred writings, that 'Except the LORD build the house, they labor in vain that build it.' I firmly believe this; and I also believe that without His recurring aid, we shall succeed in this political building no better than the builders of Babel: We shall be divided by our partial local interests; our projects will be confounded, and we ourselves shall become a reproach and a byword down to future ages. And what is worse, mankind may hereafter from this unfortunate instance, despair of establishing governments by human wisdom, and*

leave it to chance, war and conquest.

*I therefore beg leave to move - that henceforth
prayers and imploring the assistance of Heaven, and
its blessings on our deliberations, be held in this
Assembly every morning before we proceed to
business, and that one or more of the clergy of this
city be requested to officiate in that service."*

A delegate from New Jersey, Jonathan Dayton, recorded how the
representatives received the speech. He wrote:

*"The doctor sat down; and never did I behold a
countenance at once so dignified and delighted as that
of Washington at the close of the address; nor were
the members of the convention, generally, less affected.
The words of the venerable Franklin fell on our ears
with a weight and authority, even greater than we
may suppose on oracle to have had in a Roman
Senate!"*

John Witherspoon,
Founding Shepherd Of The Nation

If ever a minister of the gospel
influenced a nation, Reverend John
Witherspoon was that man. Since his
student, James Madison, became known
as *"The Father of the Constitution"*,
then certainly John Witherspoon was its
grandfather. Witherspoon was a
member of the Continental Congress
and a signer of The Declaration of
Independence. When asked if the
country was not yet ready for
independence, he tartly replied that it,
*". . . was not only ripe for the measure,
but in danger of rotting for want of it!"*

As president of the University of New Jersey, (now Princeton)
Witherspoon trained and influenced more of our Founding Fathers
than any other man. His college students included one president, a

Vice-President, three Supreme Court Justices, ten Cabinet Members, twelve Governors, twenty-one Senators, thirty-nine Congressmen and a host of delegates to the Continental Congress.

Concerning the marriage of religion and politics, Witherspoon was clear:

> *"It is in the man of piety and inward principle, that we may expect to find the uncorrupted patriot, the useful citizen, and the invincible soldier. God grant that in America true religion and civil liberty may be inseparable and that the unjust attempts to destroy the one, may in the issue tend to support and establish both.*

Notice that this statement includes a prayer that any attempt to destroy the relationship of religion and government would fall out rather to establish it. In another statement, Witherspoon's enmity toward the enemies of religious influence in America is vehement.

> *"What follows from this? That he is the best friend to American liberty, who is most sincere and active in promoting true and undefiled religion, and who sets himself with the greatest firmness to bear down profanity and immorality of every kind. Whoever is the avowed enemy of God, I scruple not to call him an enemy to his country."*

Gouverneur Morris
"We the People . . ."

The further we get from the actual events of history, the more we become subject to legends instead of history. John F. Kennedy once said that all history is legend. This is particularly true where individuals are concerned. Some characters of history grow more prominent while others are distilled from our consciousness through the inevitable attrition of limited popular memory.
Gouverneur Morris is one of the giants of the Revolutionary period

who has particularly suffered from this fate of history.

Theodore Roosevelt called Morris *"emphatically, an American first."* This is because Morris was one of the earliest of the Founding Fathers to think in terms of being *"An American"* as opposed to the more colloquial view of the time, as citizens of the various states. Morris, who served in both the Continental Congress and the Constitutional Convention, was the man responsible for the Constitution's famous preamble, which begins with, *"We the people of the United States, in order to form a more perfect Union . . ."* etc. Morris is the one who quite literally wrote the Constitution's words down on paper. It was also Morris who suggested the decimal system as the basis of our currency and coined the term *"cent"* as the basic expression for the monetary system we still use today.

Listen to what Gouverneur Morris had to say about religion, especially as it had to do with a nation's educational system.

> *"Religion is the only solid basis of good morals; therefore education should teach the precepts of religion, and the duties of man towards God."*

Here is just another example of the Founding Fathers' wisdom, which our current courts have conveniently forgotten.

Benjamin Rush
The Father of American Psychiatry

Two physicians became famous for their efforts in the defense of Boston. Dr. Joseph Warren, who died at the Battle of Breed's Hill, (and who very possibly might have eclipsed Washington) and Dr. Benjamin Rush. Rush attended the wounded after the Battles of Princeton, Brandywine, Germantown and to those who were suffering at Valley Forge. Rush was an early advocate for the Continental Congress to declare independence from Britain and was an enthusiastic signer of the Declaration of Independence.

In the realm of religion, Benjamin Rush was a devout Christian and was one of the founders of The Philadelphia Bible Society. In

1798, Dr. Rush wrote a very influential pamphlet giving twelve reasons why the Bible should be used as the central textbook in American schools. Concerning faith and the foundations of government, Rush wrote:

> *"The only foundation for a republic, is to be laid in religion. Without this there could be no virtue, and without virtue there can be no liberty, and liberty is the object and life of all republican governments."*

America's Early Educators

In addition to the clear sentiments expressed by each of these Founding Fathers, our early educators were equally clear in their views about the importance of the Bible and Christianity as the foundation of our nation's educational endeavors. A faithful representation can be seen by the following examples.

The New England Primer, The Childhood Textbook of America For Over 200 Years

The *New England Primer*, written by Benjamin Harris and printed in Boston in 1690, was, by far, the single most influential textbook in American history. The primer was designed to teach the Alphabet to children using religious maxims and moral lessons in its 90 pages. Over five million copies were printed in its lifetime, with two million of these being printed during the 1700's, our nation's founding century. In the primer, each letter of the alphabet was introduced with a rhyme, often a Biblical one, and then followed by a woodcut illustration as pictured on the previous page. The most famous children's prayer of all time first appeared in this historic textbook. We all remember it. . .

> *Now I lay me down to sleep,*
> *I pray Thee Lord, My soul to keep.*
> *If I should die before I wake,*
> *I pray Thee Lord, my soul to take.*

Many, if not most of our Founding Fathers were weaned on this sacred bedtime prayer. Now, of course, it's *"illegal"* in our schools!

Noah Webster
"In The Beginning Was The Word"

When Americans think of Noah Webster they immediately think of the enormously successful dictionary that bares his name to this day. However Noah Webster was also one of the Founding Fathers. When the Constitution was being debated in Philadelphia, Webster wrote a pamphlet to encourage its adoption. He is widely credited with being responsible for Article I, Section 8 of the finished document. After the Revolution, Webster wrote the first edition of his famous *"Blue-Backed Speller"* which went through 385 editions in his lifetime and eventually sold over sixty million copies. He followed this up with *a grammar,* (1784) and *a reader,* (1785) and an early dictionary, (1806) His most lasting work, *An American Dictionary of the English Language* was finally published in 1828. In the preface to the first edition, Webster wrote:

> *"In my view, the Christian religion is the most important and one of the earliest things in which all children, under a free government ought to be instructed. . . No truth is more evident to my mind than that the Christian religion must be the basis of any government intended to secure the rights and privileges of a free people."*

Jedediah Morse
The Father of American Geography

Jedediah Morse gave America its first glimpse of itself by producing *The American Gazetteer*, which was a kind of early *National Geographic*-style almanac which included seven large fold out maps and seven thousand articles on various places. The volume was so successful that it enjoyed 25 reprints. His early textbook, *Geography Made Easy* (1784) became an American standard in its field, and his *Annals of the American Revolution*, (1824) places him foremost among the chroniclers of our nation's founding struggle. Morse wrote the following observations about the influence of Christianity upon freedom.

> *"To the kindly influence of Christianity we owe that degree of civil freedom, and political and social happiness which mankind now enjoys. In proportion as the genuine effects of Christianity are diminished in any nation. . . in the same proportion will the people of that nation recede from the blessings of genuine freedom. . . All efforts to destroy the foundations of holy religion, ultimately tend to the subversion also of our political freedom and happiness. Whenever the pillars of Christianity shall be overthrown, our present republican forms of government, and all the blessings which flow from them, must fall with them."*

William Holmes McGuffey,
America's Schoolmaster

Reverend William Holmes McGuffey was an American educator and textbook writer. The success of his *Readers* is unparalleled in American History, selling over 122 million copies. You might say that America became great through the children that were educated on the *McGuffey Readers*. McGuffey explained the truth of our history and the basis of his textbook in the following statement.

"The Christian Religion is the religion of our country. From it are derived our notions on the character of God, on the great moral Governor of the universe. On its doctrines are founded the peculiarities of our free institutions. From no source has the author drawn more conspicuously than from the sacred Scriptures. For all these extracts from the Bible I make no apology."

Will Rogers,
America's Ambassador of Common Sense

Will Rogers isn't exactly a Founding Father, but he was as close to being an *"unofficial spokesman"* for the average American as you could find. Will once joked, *"I went through McGuffey's Fourth Grade Reader so many times, that I knew it better than McGuffey did."* In Oklahoma, we're pretty proud of the product.

I close with a 1927 quote by Will Rogers that pretty much sums up what this lesson is all about. In a comment concerning Russia, ten years after the communist revolution, Will wrote:

"Nobody knows what the outcome in Russia will be or how long this government will last. But if they do get by for a while on everything else, they picked the only one thing I know of to suppress that is absolutely necessary to run a country on, and that is religion."

Will obviously knew what he was talking about because today, the Soviet Union is long dead. Unfortunately, thanks to fifty years of renegade court rulings, America is headed for the same fate if we don't reverse gears and start instilling spiritual values in the hearts of our children. We can do this; after all, we are the children of our Pilgrim Fathers. Let us rise up, therefore, and reaffirm our faith in the God of our fathers! My fellow Americans, it is not yet too late!

Lesson Two: Open Book Quiz
(See how much you can remember. The answers are on page 243)

1. Fill in the blanks in this quote from John Jay, our nation's first Chief Justice: "*It is the* _____ *as well as the privilege and interest of our* _____ *nation to select and prefer* _____ *for their rulers.*"

2. Who said: "*It cannot be emphasized too strongly or too often that this great nation was founded, not by religionists, but by Christians; not on religions, but on the Gospel of Jesus Christ!* "? _____
_____

3. Who said: *Providence punishes national sins, by national calamities.*"? _____

4. Who said: "*I have lived Sir, a long time, and the longer I live, the more convincing proofs I see of this great truth - 'That God governs in the affairs of men.' And if a sparrow cannot fall to the ground without His notice, is it probable that an empire can rise without His aid?* " _____

5. Who said: "*God grant that in America true religion and civil liberty may be inseparable and that the unjust attempts to destroy the one, may in the issue tend to support and establish both.*" ? _____
_____

6. Fill in the blanks in this quote by Gouverneur Morris: " _____ *is the only solid basis of good morals; therefore* _____ *should teach the precepts of* _____, *and the duties of man towards* _____.*"

7. Fill in the blanks in this quote by Benjamin Rush: "*The only foundation for a republic, is to be laid in* _____. *Without this there could be no virtue, and without virtue there can be no* _____.*"

8. What is the name of the school textbook that included the famous childhood prayer which begins: "*Now I lay me down to sleep?* " ____
_____

9. Which Founding Father wrote: *The Christian religion is the most important and one of the earliest things in which all children, under a free government ought to be instructed.*"? _____

The Original 1814 Star Spangled Banner

Lesson Three
Our National Songs
The Testimony of Our National Songs, Our National Motto, and Our Pledge of Allegiance

In our first two lessons, we examined our nation's spiritual heritage as faithfully represented in the quotes of our Presidents and Founding Fathers. In this lesson, we will explore the testimony of our national songs and so on. The imprint is unmistakably God-centered

When God Came To America's Defense

By 1814, The War of 1812 was looking desperate for the new American republic. The outlook appeared quite different when Congress had declared war on England in 1812. At that time, both the British Army and Navy were preoccupied in a deadly continental struggle with France. But, that had all now changed. The British had just vanquished the armies of Napoleon, and with the blood lust of victory still fresh and sweet upon their lips, the crown finally turned its full attention to dealing with America's thirty-six year-old rebellion. It appeared to all observers that England was finally poised to enjoy her long awaited revenge. Britain's mighty navy and 18,000 seasoned troops were sent to humiliate and utterly defeat the American embarrassment, once and for all.

By mid-1814, the Americans had lost battle after battle. Canada was a total loss. The Americans then lost Mackinaw and Dearborn, and, to add insult to injury, Detroit, along with its 2000 troops surrendered without firing a single shot. Things in America looked bleak indeed. In this war, unlike the now distant revolution, the untrained American militias did not have the French to come to their aid. Worst of all, they had no one like George Washington to lead their troops. The citizens of the United States were genuinely terrified. However, what happened in Washington, D. C. on August 25, so demoralized the English army that it would never, ever taste victory on American soil again. For the first time in history, a conquering army would be totally humiliated *in* victory. This is the true story.

The Chesapeake Invasion

On August 19, 1814, the British fleet landed at Benedict, Maryland in Chesapeake Bay. British Vice-Admiral Alexander Cochrane, nursing a thirty-six year old personal vendetta against America, ordered the destruction of every assailable village along the Chesapeake. *"I want to give the Americans a complete drubbing,"* he boasted. British Vice-Admiral George Cockburn carried out Cochrane's orders with brutal efficiency. British troops burned, plundered and raped their way up the Chesapeake in a terrorizing drive toward Washington and Baltimore.

Under the command of Major-General Robert Ross, the British marched 5000 troops to within six miles of the nation's capitol, where, in less than one hour, it soundly routed 7000 hastily assembled American militiamen at the Battle of Bladensburg. The routing was so complete that the retreat of the Americans, and the hot pursuit of the British came to be known among the British as *"The Bladensburg Races".* When the British crossed the north branch of the Potomac River, they saw the unprotected capital stretched out helpless before them. As one historian wrote, *"The capital city lay defenseless before the British like tethered prey."*

When Vice-Admiral George Cockburn entered the city around eight o'clock in the evening, he ascended Capitol Hill like a peacock where the officers held a mock session of Congress. A unanimous resolution was promptly passed to torch every public building within the nation's capitol. One eyewitness observed: *"No drawing room was ever as brilliantly lit as the whole city that night."*

After burning the Capitol Building, the British then moved on toward The White House where they arrived around ten o'clock. As they entered the Executive Mansion, they found an abandoned dinner fully prepared on elegantly set tables. This, the officers ate as they mockingly drank to *"Jimmy's health,"* in derision of America's little 100-pound President, James Madison.

After dinner, Admiral Cockburn ordered his troops to stack the furniture in each of the mansion's rooms and to soak them with oil from The White House lamps. At about one o'clock in the morning, as Lieutenant Pratt fired his pistol, lighted javelins were thrown through every window of the mansion's lower floor. The mansion exploded into flames. A British eyewitness, a Mrs. Thornton, boasted: *"It glowed like a great plumb cake."* Others reported that the burning capitol could be seen from fifty miles away.

A broken hearted President Madison could only watch in disbelief from the Virginia side of the Potomac. Militia private, George Douglas, voiced the sentiment of all his countrymen when he wrote: *"Every American heart is bursting with shame and indignation at the catastrophe."* The pride of the United States was humbled in one single terrifying night. Many Americans openly wept. . . others began to pray.

Woodcut depicting the burning of The White House early on August 25, 1814

Divine Retribution

As the morning of August 25 began to dawn, the British, drunk with the wine of victory, returned again to their destructive work, setting the remaining public buildings afire. As they set the Office of War ablaze, they hardly noticed as the clouds began to darken.

Suddenly, and with very little warning, lightening split the clouds as a deafening thunder rolled across the city. For over two hours, gale-force winds blew as a torrential downpour raged against the British troops, dousing all the flames. One British soldier wrote:

> *"Our column was completely dispersed, as if it had received a total defeat. Some of the men went flying for shelter behind walls and buildings, and others, falling flat upon the ground to prevent themselves from being carried away. Such was the violence of the wind that two pieces of cannon were fairly lifted from the ground and borne several feet away."*

One officer, who refused to dismount, was thrown horse and rider flat against the ground. The force of the wind was so violent that the heavy chain bridge across the Potomac buckled and was rendered useless. Martin O'Mally, two-term mayor of the City of Baltimore, stated in 2004:

> *"We now know that a tornado actually touched down, like the mighty wrathful hand of God from the Old Testament and afflicted more casualties in the middle of that British column than they had suffered at Bladensburg."*

Admiral Cockburn is said to have asked a lady resident of Washington, *"Madam, is this the kind of storm that you are accustomed to in this infernal country?"* To which she replied, *"No Sir, this is a special interposition of Providence, to drive our enemies from our city!"*

The British retreated that evening in a state of confusion and bewilderment. This would be the last British victory of any kind upon American soil. The next battle would give birth to our great national anthem.

The Battle of Baltimore

News of the capitol's burning spread like wildfire across America. News also of the great storm traveled with it. Americans everywhere were drawn together in unity and in prayer, much like modern America was after 9/11. News reached Baltimore too, where it became obvious that it would be the next major target of the British. Every heart in Baltimore was filled with fear. The ministers of the city issued a call to prayer even as defensive measures were set into motion.

General Samuel Smith, a veteran of the Revolutionary War, and now of the Maryland Militia, was assigned the task of preparing for the defense of Baltimore. He began in earnest to build a mile of earthen entrenchments at Baltimore's eastern approaches. The shipping merchants sacrificed their entire fleet as they sunk their own vessels to form a blockade reef across the entrance to Baltimore Harbor.

Meanwhile, the task of defending Fort McHenry was given to thirty-eight-year-old George Armistead. Here, one quarter-of-a-million pounds of gunpowder, a major portion of the nation's supply, lay stockpiled and protected. Fort McHenry was also critical because it defended the harbor against enemy naval attack. If Fort McHenry were to fall, Baltimore could not be saved. Fifty-seven cannons were positioned on the ramparts of the fort.

"We are ready, except that we have no suitable ensign." Armistead reported, *"It is my desire to have a flag so large that the British will have no difficulty seeing it."*

Photo courtesy of The National Park Service

Strangely enough, the fort that became famous for the Star Spangled Banner, was itself built in the form of a star. The fort was also established in 1776, the year of our nation's birth.

The Star Spangled Flag

Mary Pickersgill must go down in history alongside Betsy Ross because of her tireless efforts to produce *"a proper ensign"*, which came to be known as The Star Spangled Banner. Actually, Armistead ordered two flags; one was a very large garrison flag of woolen bunting and cotton stars, and a smaller storm flag to fly during battle. The larger flag measured thirty by forty-two feet, with the stars measuring two feet across. Mary Pickersgill, her daughter, Caroline, and several other ladies worked tirelessly to complete the flag in the given time. Records show that they were paid $574.44 for the two flags.

By Land And By Sea

At noon on September 11, an alarm cannon sounded as the British were sighted in the distance. A force of some fifty British vessels, including 16 warships and 4000 troops combined to execute a simultaneous land and sea assault upon the city. On September 12, as General Ross was staging his troops from the east, American General, John Stricker unexpectedly went forward to harass him outside of Baltimore. During this surprise skirmish General Ross rushed forward to assess the strength of the American assault. Just then, an unknown American sniper shot and killed the British Commander. Shockwaves passed through the British regiments. Was this another Divine interposition? Washington's *"perfect storm"* was still fresh in the minds of the men. The British morale began to show fear and fatigue.

Nevertheless, the British commanders decided to move forward with their battle plans. In the wee morning hours of September 13, British gunships named *Terror, Meteor, Devastation, Volcano* and others unleashed an 1814-version of *"shock and awe"* upon the one thousand defenders of Fort McHenry. One observer of the time stated: *"Never, from the time of the invention of the cannon to present day, were the same number of pieces fired with so rapid succession."* The smaller guns of the fort could not reach the anchored gunboats of the British fleet. The defenders of Fort McHenry could only stand their ground, refuse to abandon the fort, and pray.

At about three o'clock in the afternoon, the British gunboats moved closer, as if to finish off the last of the fort's defenders. They soon discovered that the guns of Fort McHenry were still well manned and could speak with an unmistakably lethal retort. The British resumed their safer positions and the bombardment continued throughout the night of September 13-14. During the assault, somewhere between 1,500 and 1,800, 220-pound bombs and 700 rockets were hurled at the fort. Inside, the defenders crouched behind the walls only to have the bombs explode over their heads and behind them, the shrapnel of which was both devastating and terrorizing. One soldier later wrote: *"We were like pigeons, tied by the leg to be shot at."* One bomb actually penetrated pell-mell into the very midst of the fort's quarter-of-a-million pounds of gunpowder, but miraculously, failed to explode.

By Dawn's Early Light

As the heavy barrage continued through the night, an American lawyer by the name of Francis Scott Key and an associate watched from the decks of the British frigate, *H.M.S. Surprise*, captained by the son of Vice-Admiral Cochrane. On official business, Key had been detained until after the battle was decided. All through the night

the two Americans anxiously kept a watch, hoping and praying that his fellow Americans would not surrender the fort. As long as they continued to see the flag flying, they knew that the fort's defenders remained defiant. By *"the rockets red glare, and bombs bursting in air"* they occasionally caught glimpses of the flag through the night. On the morning of the 14th, the British guns fell silent. A haze of smoke and an early morning mist shrouded Fort McHenry from view. Quietly, anxiously, they strained to see the verdict.

Woodcut of Francis Scott Key spying the Star Spangled Banner after the overnight bombardment of Ft. McHenry.

Meanwhile at the fort, Major Armistead, realizing that the sun was rising, ordered his men to take down the smaller storm flag and hoist the huge garrison flag. As a gentle morning breeze cleared the mist, the British had *"no trouble seeing the flag"*. One British observer noted that they beheld, *"A most superb and splendid ensign flying over the battery!"*

When Francis Scott Key saw the flag of America flying grander than ever, he was moved with emotion. He later wrote, of his feelings at the time. He said:

> *"I saw the flag of my country waving over a city,*
> *the strength and the pride of my native state. And does*
> *not such a country, and such defenders of their country,*
> *deserve a song?"*

Then, taking an envelope from his pocket, he began to pen the now famous words of what has since become America's National Anthem. Because Fort McHenry had not capitulated, and because the land assault had likewise faltered, the British, withdrew in humiliation and shame. To continue the fight was pointless. Only one more attempt would ever be made by the British to make headway against the Americans, the Battle of New Orleans. There, under the command of General Andrew Jackson, the British were soundly defeated, losing over 2000 men to the American's thirteen.

Key, along with the help of some friends, had the poem printed and distributed in Baltimore with a note that it should be sung to the popular tune: *Anacreon In Heaven.*

Monument to Francis Scott Key in Baltimore, Maryland

Photo courtesy of The Maryland Historical Society

The Rest of the Story

Do we really know anything about Francis Scott Key, and do we really know the message of our own national anthem? Why did Americans universally embrace this song? And why did Congress officially adopt it as our National Anthem in 1931? Who exactly was Francis Scott Key and what message does his song, yea, our national anthem, convey?

Francis Scott Key, a Georgetown lawyer, had been present at the burning of Washington just two weeks earlier. Seeing the glow from Georgetown, Key, who was a volunteer in the Virginia Light Artillery, refused to leave with his wife and family, feeling it was his duty to remain behind. It was from here that he was later dispatched by orders of President Madison to seek the release of Dr. William Beanes, who had been accused of being a spy. It was because of this mission that he came to be in Baltimore and an eyewitness of the bombardment of Fort McHenry.

Key was undeniably a very devout Christian. Earlier in life, he had seriously considered becoming a minister. He was a founding trustee of his church's General Theological Seminary, and so remained until his death. Excepting 1814, because of the war, Key never missed one of his church's annual general assemblies. Key also wrote many other religious poems and two Christian hymns that are used during church worship even today. They are: *Before the Lord We Bow*, and, *Lord With Glowing Heart I'd Praise Thee.* The religious and spiritual message of his song, *The Star Spangled Banner*, is no less evident.

Key later wrote what was going through his mind during the Battle of Fort McHenry:

> *"I could not feel a hope that they would escape. And again, when I thought of the many faithful, whose piety (religious sincerity) leavens the lump of wickedness, I could hardly feel a fear."*

Concerning the outcome of the battle he went on to write:

> *"It seems to have given me a higher idea of the forbearance, long-suffering and tender mercy of God than I have ever before received."*

Our National Anthem

Most of us know, and can even sing the first verse of *The Star Spangled Banner*, but do we know the last verse, the verse that summarizes the song, and the verse that gave us our national motto? Here it is. What do you think the message of the last verse is?

> *O thus be it ever when free men shall stand,*
> *Between their lov'd home, and war's desolation,*
> *Blest with vict'ry and peace, may the Heav'n rescued land,*
> *Praise the Pow'r that hath made and preserved us a nation.*
> *Then conquer we must, when our cause it is just,*
> *And this be our motto: "In God is our trust".*
> *And the Star-Spangled Banner in triumph shall wave*
> *O'er the land of the free, and the home of the brave.*

Is it not obvious, that this is not only a patriotic song, but a spiritual song as well? After all, that's what an anthem, by definition is: *"A sacred vocal composition"*. Thus, when Congress officially adopted *The Star Spangled Banner* as our National Anthem in 1931, (for the people had already adopted it in their hearts long before) they were giving us a national hymn, not about a flag, but for what the flag stood for; that we were one nation that sincerely trusted in God. That is why our flag is so sacred to Americans. Our flag stands for a national trust in Almighty God. This is why President Dwight Eisenhower could say:

> *"Without God, there could be no American form of government, nor an American way of life. Recognition of the Supreme Being is the first, the most basic expression of Americanism."*

This is why burning the flag is one of the worst violations of our American ideals. In 1916, President Woodrow Wilson, a devout Christian, ordered that *The Star Spangled Banner* should become the national anthem played by the military and naval services. However, it was not until 1931, during the administration of Herbert Hoover, that Congress officially designated it as our national anthem with these words:

> *"Be it enacted by the Senate and House of Representatives of the United States of America in Congress assembled, That the composition known as The Star Spangled Banner is designated as the National Anthem of the United States of America."*

Our National Motto

Although a proposed seal containing the words, *E Pluribus Unum* was originally rejected, a modified version of the seal was adapted in 1792. However, these particular words were never officially sanctioned as our national motto per se. However, as a result of the popularity of Key's song, and through the tireless efforts of Reverend M. R. Watkinson and many other ministers, Key's proposed motto was shortened to *"In God We Trust"* and first appeared on the newly designed two cent piece in 1864 with approval of the U.S. Congress.

Then, in 1956, under the administration of President Dwight D. Eisenhower, the 84th Congress of the United States officially designated the words, *"In God We Trust"* as our national motto. To date there have been at least four serious challenges to the constitutionality of the motto, but, thank God, it has successfully withstood each challenge although the rationale of the rulings have set dangerous precedents for future cases.

Our Pledge of Allegiance

Our pledge of allegiance evolved from its first appearance in *The Youth's Companion* magazine, dated September 8, 1892, in which it appeared in anticipation of the 400th anniversary of Columbus's discovery of America. It was published anonymously and without copyright. To this day there is a controversy over who actually penned the original words. However, there is no controversy as to who added the two words, *"Under God"* to the pledge. On June 14th, (Flag Day) 1954, President Dwight Eisenhower approved a congressional measure, which officially added the words, *"Under God"* as part of the official version, previously approved on June 22, 1942. In approving the change, President Eisenhower said:

> *"In this way we are reaffirming the transcendence of religious faith in America's heritage and future. In this way we shall constantly strengthen those spiritual weapons which forever will be our country's most powerful resource in peace and war."*

We must thank God and defend the legacy that both our Founding Fathers and those who followed have left us in this great spiritual legacy.

Our Other National Songs

Although this chapter, of necessity, has already grown lengthy, I feel that we cannot close until we allow our other national songs to bear witness to the spiritual foundations and heritage of our nation. Did you know that the song, *God Bless America* is written in the form of a prayer and that it refers to God three times? Did you know that *The Star Spangled Banner* also refers to God three times? *America the Beautiful* refers to Him four times. *My Country Tis of Thee (America)* references God seven times. And, *The Battle Hymn of the Republic refers* to God or the gospel twenty-three times! Let's take a quick look at each of these in the order they were written.

My Country 'Tis of Thee (America)

This wonderful and beloved song has been called *"America's unofficial national anthem"*. It is sung *of* America, *(of thee I sing)* but it is sung *to* our fathers' God, *(to Thee we sing)*. The first three stanzas extol the glory of America's landscape, freedom and forebears, while the last stanza breaks forth in a beautiful prayer to America's *"Great God our King"*.

America, as it was originally called, was written in 1832 by a twenty-four year-old theological student named Samuel Francis Smith. It took him only thirty minutes to write the words on a scrap piece of paper. Sung to the tune of England's *God Save the King*, it became an instant success. After graduation from Harvard and then Andover Seminary, Smith became a successful minister of the gospel, serving in several Baptist churches in the eastern part of the United States. During his eighty-seven years on earth, he composed over 150 other hymns and served as Secretary of the Baptist Missionary Union.

My Country, 'Tis of Thee
By Samuel Francis Smith, 1832

My country, 'tis of thee,
Sweet land of liberty
Of thee I sing;
Land where my fathers died,
Land of the pilgrims' pride,
From every mountain side
Let freedom ring.

My native country, thee,
Land of the noble free,
Thy name I love;
I love thy rocks and rills,
Thy woods and templed hills,
My heart with rapture thrills
Like that above.

Let music swell the breeze,
And ring from all the trees
Sweet freedom's song;
Let mortal tongue awake;
Let all that breathe partake;
Let rocks their silence break,
The sound prolong.

Our fathers' God to Thee,
Author of Liberty,
To Thee we sing;
Long may our land be bright,
With freedom's holy light,
Protect us by Thy might
Great God, our King.

The Battle Hymn of the Republic

The Battle Hymn of the Republic is, without a doubt, one of the most inspirational of all of our national songs. It was the favorite hymn of President Ronald Reagan and was sung, not only at his funeral in 2004, but also at those of Sir Winston Churchill, Robert Kennedy and President Richard M. Nixon.

As we have said, the hymn refers to God, Christ and the gospel in one way or another some twenty-three times. This stirring hymn was written by fifty-two year-old Julia Ward Howe during the American Civil War. In one passage, the fact that it was written by a woman is reflected by way of reference to the Messianic Biblical prophecy that, *"the seed of woman"* shall crush the head of Satan. While the hymn remains quite controversial even to this day, it is undeniably beautiful and poetically rich in its metaphorical references to Christ in calling men to righteous arms.

Howe penned the song in the early morning, after visiting Union soldiers encamped along the Potomac River near Washington, D.C. She later wrote:

> *"I awoke in the gray of the morning, and as I lay waiting the dawn, the long lines of the desired poem began to entwine themselves in my mind, and I said to myself, 'I must get up and write these verses, lest I fall asleep and forget them.' So, I sprang out of the bed, and in the dimness found an old stump of a pen, which I remember using the day before. I scrawled the verses almost without looking at the paper."*

The Battle Hymn of the Republic
By Julia Ward Howe, 1862

Mine eyes have seen the glory of the coming of the Lord;
He is trampling out the vintage where the grapes of wrath are stored;
He hath loosed the fateful lightning of His terrible swift sword;
His truth is marching on.

I have seen Him in the watch fires of a hundred circling camps;
They have builded Him an altar in the evening dews and damps;
I can read His righteous sentence by the dim and flaring lamps;
His day is marching on.

He hath sounded forth the trumpet that shall never sound retreat;
He is sifting out the hearts of men before His judgement seat;
O be swift, my soul, to answer Him! Be jubilant, my feet!
Our God is marching on.

In the beauty of the lilies Christ was born across the sea,
With a glory in His bosom that transfigures you and me;
As He died to make men holy, let us die to make men free;
While God is marching on.

Chorus:
Glory! Glory, hallelujah!
Glory! Glory hallelujah!
Glory! Glory hallelujah!
His Truth is marching on
(last line of chorus matches the last line of each verse)

America the Beautiful

O Beautiful, for spacious skies, for amber waves of grain. . . Thus begins one of the most familiar and beloved of all our national songs. Like so many songs, *America the Beautiful* first appeared as a poem, which was first published in *The Congregationalist*, a religious weekly, on Independence Day, July 4, 1895.

The poem was penned by a forty-four year old instructor at Wellesley College, in Massachusetts, by the name of Katharine Lee Bates, after an inspiring trip to the top of Pikes Peak in 1893. The poem became popular to sing with many different melodies, including *Auld Lang Syne*. Katharine Bates revived the words in 1904 and again in 1913. The poem was not actually published with the tune (Materna) that we are familiar with today until 1910.

The song is especially rich because it not only celebrates the vast beauty of America's landscape, but because its message is one that acknowledged God's grace as the primary reason for America's greatness. The song also acknowledges the need for unselfishness, self-control, brotherhood, and the need for liberty to be rooted in and restrained by the rule of moral laws.

America, the Beautiful
By Katharine Lee Bates, 1893

O beautiful for spacious skies, for amber waves of grain.
For purple mountain majesties, above the fruited plain!
America! America! God shed His grace on thee,
And crown thy good with brotherhood, from sea to shining sea.

O beautiful for pilgrim feet, whose stern, impassioned stress,
A thoroughfare, for freedom beat, across the wilderness!
America! America! God mend thine ev'ry flaw,
Confirm thy soul, in self-control, thy liberty in law.

O beautiful for heroes proved in liberating strife,
Who more than self, their country loved, and mercy more than life.
America! America! May God thy gold refine,
Till all success be nobleness, and every gain Divine.

O beautiful for patriot dream that sees beyond the years
Thine alabaster cities gleam, undimmed by human tears!
America! America! God shed His grace on thee,
And crown thy good with brotherhood from sea to shining sea.

God Bless America

Few people would believe it if you told them that Irving Berlin could neither read nor write music, yet, along with so many other musical treasures, his patriotic song, *God Bless America* is one of our nation's most cherished songs.

The song, which is actually a prayer set to music, was first written in the summer of 1918, but was set aside because it was thought to be too solemn in tone for the musical production he was then composing. However, as war loomed over Europe in the fall of 1938, Berlin was asked to compose a patriotic song for Kate Smith to sing on Armistice Day. After a few failed attempts, Berlin remembered his song, *God Bless America* from some twenty years earlier. After some alterations, singer Kate Smith electrified the nation with its first broadcast performance over the radio on Armistice Day, November 11, 1938. The song was an instant sensation and has been ever since. (Note: copyright laws prohibit us from reproducing this song here)

God Bless the U.S.A.

No overview of America's spiritual patriotic songs would be complete without including a look at the twenty-three year-old phenomena of singer/songwriter, Lee Greenwood's blockbuster hit song, *God Bless the U.S.A.*

If anyone ever doubted that old-fashioned patriotism was still alive in today's America, the reception that Lee Greenwood's song received from his countrymen, should lay this doubt to rest. I'll go a step further, if anyone doubts the power of a single song or for that matter, of a single individual to make a difference, Greenwood and his song should silence those doubts.

Photo courtesy of The U. S. Air Force, Yoland Hunter, Photographer

Lee Greenwood is more than just a singer, songwriter and entertainer; when you examine his words, you'll find they reveal a man of deep faith and spiritual understanding. Lee is a Christian patriot who rightfully belongs in the same league as Francis Scott Key. His song ministers to a different time, our time, but it goes just as deep if not deeper into the spiritual soul of America as our national anthem does. The instant and enduring popularity of Greenwood's song is a testament to the fact that we are still the children of our fathers, and that we, as a country, still embrace the faith of our fathers. Concerning his song, *God Bless the U.S.A.*, Greenwood said: *"Having this song with God in it appeal to so many Americans helps me think that God is still protecting America. I certainly hope so."* What does he feel when he performs the song? *"It's always a spiritual experience. It's not just American; it is not just patriotism."* As far as his song's message and impact is concerned, Greenwood added, *"That's why I believe that we must never fail to affirm that we are indeed one nation under God."* This statement pretty well sums this chapter up. (Note: copyright laws prohibit us from reproducing the song here)

Prayer Force One

Not long ago, I also wrote a song, not surprisingly entitled: *Prayer Force One.* While I do not mean to appear presumptuous by including my song along with the great American songs included in this chapter, I present it as a reflection of my heart's dream for an America, united in prayer. I offer this song to God and America with the prayer that it will be a blessing to all those who would sing or hear it.

I am grateful to Dale Griffin of Oklahoma Baptist University for taking the time to transcribe the music from a cassette tape on which I sang the song. It must have been an ordeal for him to be sure. We are currently working to have both an instrumental and voice version recorded. It is our intention of making it available on our web site and that it might be downloaded by those who wish to perform the song in their churches.

Prayer Force One, words and music copyright, 2007 by Ed Moore

The complete song including all three stanzas and chorus are printed on the next page. If you would like a printable copy of the words or music, please visit our web site at <PrayerForceOne.com>.

Prayer Force One
By Ed Moore

First Stanza:

There's a way to save our wounded land today;
If we'll join hands and kneel and humbly pray;
Confess our sins, and seek God's face today;
When we join hands, when we are one,
We're *Prayer Force One*.

Chorus:

Prayer Force One, Prayer Force One;
When we join hands,
We're *Prayer Force One*. . .
And our God will hear, and heal our land;
When we join hands, when we are one,
We're *Prayer Force One*.

Second Stanza:

Put not your trust in chariots or men;
But trust in the LORD our God again;
Believe His Word, and lift up prayerful hands;
When we join hands, when we are one,
We're *Prayer Force One*

Third Stanza:

There is no force on earth that we must fear;
When we do right and pray, our LORD is near;
"In God We Trust" are words we all hold dear;
When we join hands, when we are one,
We're *Prayer Force One*.

Lesson Three: Open Book Quiz

(See how much you can remember. The answers are on page 244)

1. What drove the British from Washington D.C. on August 25th, 1814? _____

2. What fort refused to surrender, thus inspiring our national anthem? _____

3. What lawyer/hymn-writer gave us our national anthem? _____ _____ _____

4. What famous song first suggested that our national motto should be *"In God Is Our Trust"*?_____

5. In what year was *The Star Spangled Banner* officially designated as our national anthem? _____

6. In what year, and under who's administration did the words, *"In God We Trust"* first appear on an American coin? (year) _____ (president) _____.

7. Fill in the blanks of President Eisenhower's quote as he approved adding the words, *"Under God"* to our Pledge of Allegiance. *"In this way we are reaffirming the transcendence of _____ _____ in America's heritage and future. In this way we shall constantly strengthen those _____ weapons which forever will be our country's most powerful _____ in peace and war."*

8. How many references to God, Christ and the Gospel are there in *The Battle Hymn of the Republic*? _____

9. In the song, *America the Beautiful*, what are we told that God shed on America? _____ _____

10. According to the fourth stanza, to whom is the song *My Country Tis of Thee* directed? _____ _____ _____

11. What four leaders had *The Battle Hymn of the Republic* sung at their funerals? _____
_____
_____
_____

12. *God Bless America* is written in the form of a _____.

13. Complete this statement by Lee Greenwood, *"That's why I believe that we must never fail to_____ that we are indeed one nation under _____."*

Colonial patriot showing respect to the Christian Cross and the Ten Commandments, in front of the U.S. District Court Building in Washington, D.C.

Lesson Four
Our Nation's Legacy In Stone
As Preserved In Our National Architecture

Why did our forebears sculpt and engrave our national monuments and architecture with religious images and words? They did, you know! In fact, these religious images are everywhere and in every state. Our nation's capitol, Washington D.C., is literally enshrined with them. How did this happen and why was it done?

The answer to these questions lies in the long history of man. Throughout the story of man, each generation has sought to leave their collective wisdom carved in stone, as a legacy to their children and to their children's children. They did this because they did not want their children to forget what they had learned. Not all nations have legacies worth leaving. For example, the founders of the former Soviet Union sought to enshrine evil men and their vile utterances in stone, in order to preserve the enslavement of their people. They erected huge statues of such men as Karl Marx, Vladimir Lennin and Joseph Stalin; only to have their children pull them down in utter contempt.

On the other side of the political spectrum, free nations, likc the United States, England and many others, have sought to preserve the legacy of freedom through vital documents and by engraving them on granite buildings.

The History of National Monuments and Engravings

As I have said, the desire to pass a nation's legacy on to its children is not new. One of the oldest examples is to be found in the first book of the Bible, Genesis. Here, Jacob and his father-in-law, Laban, made a covenant of peace, attested to by a pillar of stone. In Genesis 31:44-49a & 52, we read:

165

*"Now therefore come and let us make a covenant,
I and thou; and let it be for a witness between me and
thee. And Jacob took a stone, and set it up for a pillar.*

*And Jacob said unto his brethren, 'Gather stones;
and they took stones and made an heap: and they did
eat there upon the heap. And Laban called it
Jegarsahadutha: but Jacob called it Galeed.* (In both
languages it means, 'The heap of witness'.)

*And Laban said, 'This heap is a witness between
me and thee this day'. Therefore was the place called
Galeed and Mizpah...* (which means 'a beacon')

*This heap be a witness, and this pillar be a witness,
that I will not pass over this heap to thee, and that
thou shalt not pass over this heap and this pillar unto
me for harm."*

Here we can see that such monuments were used as sacred seals
to solemn covenants. As in this story, these were often pillars of stone,
built to witness and commemorate solemn events. Eventually, these
monuments came to serve as lasting reminders, built for the benefit
of generations to come. We can see a Bible example of this in Joshua
4:1-7 we read:

*"And it came to pass, when all the people were
clean passed over Jordan, that the LORD spake unto
Joshua, saying, Take you twelve men out of the people,
out of every tribe a man, and command ye them,
saying, 'Take you hence out of the midst of Jordan,
out of the place where the priests' feet stood firm,
twelve stones, and ye shall carry them over with you,
and leave them in the lodging place, where ye shall
lodge this night'.*

*Then Joshua called the twelve men, whom he had
prepared of the children of Israel, out of every tribe a
man: and Joshua said unto them, 'Pass over before
the ark of the LORD your God into the midst of Jordan,
and take you up every man of you a stone upon his
shoulder, according to the number of the tribes of the*

children of Israel: that this may be a sign among you, that when your children shall ask their fathers in time to come, saying, 'What mean ye by these stones?' Then ye shall answer them, 'That the waters of Jordan were cut off before the ark of the covenant of the LORD; when it passed over Jordan, the waters of Jordan were cut off': and these stones shall be for a memorial unto the children of Israel for ever."

Here, we can see that Joshua was acting upon the instructions of God, for God knew that future generations would have a propensity to forget His laws and embrace sin. These simple stones were to become a memorial to remind Israel's descendants of what God had done for them.

In the process of time, these ancient covenant stones came to be called landmarks, for they marked sacred covenants and events all across the landscape. In fact it became a sin for one to deface or remove one of these *"witnesses to history"* and the promises they represented. This is why the Bible forbade the destruction of any such landmark. The Bible says: *"Remove not the ancient landmark, which thy fathers have set."* (Proverbs 22:28), for to do so was to destroy the historic testimony of the fathers, and of the binding covenants which they had made.

> *"Remove not the ancient landmark, which thy fathers have set." (Proverbs 22:28)*

On a common level, these covenant stones became known as landmarks because they served to mark boundaries where territorial land agreements had been reached. This is why the Law of Moses plainly stated:

"Thou shalt not remove thy neighbor's landmark, which they of old time have set in thine inheritance, which thou shalt inherit in the land that the LORD thy God giveth thee to possess it."

(Deuteronomy 19:14)

Where great landmarks of national importance were concerned, it became a national sin to deface or destroy such a covenant stone or monument. As time progressed, and the advent of lasting architecture developed, it became natural for civilizations to immortalize their leaders and the foundations of their cultures by engraving them in the stones of their great architectural edifices. Naturally, national governments were nearly always at the forefront of these efforts.

The Advent of American Ideals

Then came the American Republic. Never before had such a moment in history occurred. America was born at a time, when, all of the history of men and governments lay preserved before the founders; when freedom's struggle was at a crossroads of destiny; and when Christian principles were never more highly esteemed and almost universally embraced by the people. Those few decades of history were to give birth to the United States of America, and all of the high ideals upon which a free world would emerge.

In an effort to preserve these ideals as the foundations upon which the nation had been built, the public buildings of America's architectural landscape were erected to bear testimony of these origins. These buildings, monuments, memorials and public shrines have captured the truth of our nation's origins for all generations of Americans to come. Let us briefly examine the testimony of our fathers as preserved for us in stone.

Photo courtesy of Carrie Devorah

ABOVE: Moses and The Ten Commandments in the center of the facade on the United States Supreme Court Building

Moses and The Ten Commandments

One of the most obvious and oft occurring images that we find in our public architecture is that of Moses and The Ten Commandments. The reason for this is that the Law of Moses was considered by our founding fathers to be the foundation for all moral law. It was

ABOVE: A carving of The Ten Commandments on the door of the United States Supreme Court

never the intent of the founding fathers that freedom of worship would be so construed as to mean freedom *from* the influence of religion as the basis for moral law. The history of the founding period overwhelmingly bears this out. Our forefathers knew that there had to be a moral foundation for law. Otherwise, the very lack of such a foundation, itself, would become the foundation for any and every kind of evil and immoral behavior. It was no accident that the United States was founded upon a reverent recognition that all civil law must be based on Divine law. This is why our founding documents and writings of the founders again and again refer to God and His law.

Therefore, in order to preserve

ABOVE: Moses and The Ten Commandments inside the courtroom of the United States Supreme Court

ABOVE: Moses and the Ten Commandments in the Library of Congress, Washington, D.C.

Photo courtesy of Carrie Devorah

this legacy for their children, our leaders engraved many images of Moses and the Ten Commandments on our government buildings. The very edifice, which houses the Supreme Court of the United States, bears testimony to the religious foundation of our laws. Here, Moses and the Ten Commandments are depicted at the center, preeminent position on the facade of the Supreme Court Building. (shown on page 130) Likewise, to enter into the courtroom, one must pass

Photo courtesy of Carrie Devorah

ABOVE: The Ten Commandments on the floor of the National Archieves

through a door with a carving of the Ten Commandments. (shown on top of page 131) Then, once inside the courtroom, you will again see the sculptured image of Moses and The Ten Commandments. (shown at bottom of page 131)

ABOVE: A portion of President Abraham Lincoln's Second Inaugural Address, containing five highlighted references to God.

The Supreme Court Building is not the only place you will find images of The Ten Commandments. Also pictured on these pages, you will find such depictions in or on the National Archives, the Library of Congress, and the United States District Court. (And there are many others not pictured.)

Other Religious Images

There are of course, many other images preserved in our national architecture that bear witness to the foundations of our nation. One of my personal favorites is the *Adams Prayer Mantle* in The White House. I've already told the story of how this prayer is the first recorded act of any president in The White House.

Ed Moore

President Franklin Delano Roosevelt was so thoroughly taken with this prayer, that he had it engraved on the mantle of the State Dining Room of The White House. Later, when President Harry Truman had the White House gutted and restored during his administration, he made sure that the mantle was carefully copied and replaced. (The original is now on display at the Harry S. Truman Presidential Library and Museum. (To read the text of the prayer, turn to page 110)

Our next photograph is of the chapel in the U. S. Capitol Building. The inscription at the top of the window reads, *"This Nation Under God"*, and the verse quoted, is from the book of Psalms, chapter sixteen and verse one, which reads: *"Preserve me, O God: for in thee do I put my trust."* Is this not a beautiful picture: the *"Father of Our Country"* praying on behalf of

Stained glass window of George Washington praying. This window is in the chapel of the United States Capitol Building. The verse is Psalm 16:1, *"Preserve me, O God: for in Thee do I put my trust."*

America. Isn't it sad that there are those today, who, in the name of liberty, seek to destroy every vestige of public prayer? Would we not do well to return to the faith of our first president?

Our Presidential Monuments and Memorials

The spiritual legacy of America as represented in presidential monuments and memorials is overwhelming. It would be interesting to find out just how many times references are made to God in just these four national structures alone. (three of which are pictured below) Lincoln's short, four paragraph, Second Inaugural Address, (pictured on page 126) alone, contains no less than fifteen references to God, prayer and the Bible. Here, in the memorial dedicated to Lincoln's memory, we read his famous words: *"That this nation, under God, shall have a new birth of freedom."* The words, *"under God"* mean just that, that we are to be subject to God and to his laws; and to rely on His Divine leadership and blessings. This is a far cry from what our children are being taught in public schools today.

The Washington Monument stands 555 feet tall. It is approximately 55 feet wide at the base. The foundations are over 36 feet deep and the total weight of the structure is over 82 tons. So, what is inscribed on the monument? Other than the names and dates concerning its construction, there is only one inscription on the

TOP: The Lincoln Memorial
RIGHT: The Washington Monument
BOTTOM: The Jefferson Memorial

monument. On the east side of the monument, we find one simple Latin phrase, containing two words: *"LAUS DEO"*, which mean, *"Praise be to God."* That says it all.

In the Jefferson Memorial, we read many references to God. And it is here, etched in stone, that we find that Jefferson himself, swore, not at, but upon the altar of God.

Camp David's Evergreen Chapel

I close this chapter with a look at one of our nation's newest and least known public structures, Evergreen Chapel. Evergreen Chapel is, in effect, the personal private chapel of the President of the United States. It is located at Camp David, Maryland, where it serves as a secure place for the President and his family to worship, as well as for the benefit of the ever-changing Camp David personnel.

Like the new Air Force One, Evergreen Chapel is one of the legacies that President Ronald Reagan left to his presidential heirs. It was built with private donations to match the other rugged structures of Camp David. Again, like the new Air Force One, it was dedicated by George Herbert Walker Bush in 1991, and rededicated by his son, President George W. Bush, in 2001. The trip to Camp David is a beautiful trip along the Potomac River, about 75 miles from The White House. Most generally, however, the President arrives at Camp David aboard his marine helicopter known as Marine One. The chapel itself

Evergreen Chapel at Camp David, Maryland

has stained glass windows, two inches thick, which contain symbols that are open to the interpretation of the viewer. For instance, the mountains may be interpreted as Mt. Sinai or Mt. Calvary, or both. There are also symbols of a sheaf of wheat, the sea and anchor, the tree of knowledge, seven flames, an open book, and a dove. The officiating minister most generally determines the content of the service.

As can be readily seen from this lesson, our nation's architecture is rich in both spiritual symbolism and testimony. Just as we are admonished by scripture, not to remove the ancient landmarks of our fathers, so we must be careful to preserve it for the next generation to come. This, our fathers did for us, as a spiritual legacy in stone. Let us not forget that the most obvious inscription of all is that which our fathers minted on our U.S. coins for all the world to see: *"In God We Trust"*. But, even this is now being tampered with.

Current President and First Lady, George and Laura Bush, along with former President and First Lady, George and Barbara Bush at worship in Camp David's Evergreen Chapel, on Easter Sunday, April 6, 2006

New Presidential Dollar To Remove *"Liberty"* & Hides *"In God We Trust"*

In spite of our rich national heritage, the new Congressionally approved *"Presidential Dollar"* series will be the first U.S. coin that does not bear the word *"Liberty"* on it! To add insult to injury, it will also be the first coin to virtually *"hide"* the words, *"In God We Trust."* Instead of minting these words in a prominent place, the words will be relegated to the same place as the mint mark, on the edge of the coin!

Images Courtesy U.S. Mint

First Of The New Presidential Dollars

The new presidential dollar is due to appear about the same time as this book, (early 2007) with four different coins to be released each year until 2017. The public was not allowed to see the coin until November 20, 2006. Almost no one is aware that *"Liberty"* would not appear on the coin, nor that *"In God We Trust"* would be relegated to the edge of the coin. While we think that the public should protest these changes, we also pray that it will fall out rather to bring attention to our heritage and attempts to neutralize our national motto. We believe that it is important to continue the pattern of our godly predecessors in preserving our national heritage on our coins and public structures. We would do well to embrace the instructions of Moses when he warned Israel with these word:

> *"Only take heed to thyself, and keep thy soul diligently, lest thou forget the things which thine eyes have seen, and lest they depart from thy heart all the days of thy life: but teach them thy sons, and thy son's sons."*   (Deuteronomy 4:9)

Lesson Four: Open Book Quiz

(See how much you can remember. The answers are on page 244)

1. From earliest Biblical times we find that monuments were used as _____ seals to solemn _____.

2. In Joshua 4:7, we have an example of the fathers leaving a memorial to remind the children of Israel of the blessings of God. Fill in the blanks of the following phrase from Joshua 4:7. *"These _____ shall be for a _____."*

3. Fill in the blanks in the following commandment of God, found in Proverbs 22:28. *"Remove not the ancient _____, which thy _____ have set."*

4. On page 154, Moses and the Ten Commandments are depicted at the center of the facade of what U. S. government building? _____ _____.

5. On page 155, The Ten Commandments are depicted on the door leading into what U. S. chamber? _____

6. On page 155 Moses and The Ten Commandments are depicted inside what chamber? _____

7. What president had John Adams' first White House prayer inscribed on the fireplace mantle of the State Dining Room in the White House? _____

8. Who is depicted in prayer in the stain glass window of the Congressional Chapel in the U.S. Capitol Building? _____ _____

9. Fill in the blanks of this Lincoln quote, inscribed inside the Lincoln Memorial. *"That this nation, _____ __ _____ , shall have a new birth of freedom."*

10. What are the only two words found on the east side of the Washington Monument and what do they mean? _____ _____, (meaning) _____

11. Under what two presidents was Camp David's *Evergeen Chapel* built? _____ and _____

12. What president rededicated the Evergreen Chapel in 2001? ____ _____

13. What words are inscribed on all of our U.S. coins and currency? _____ _____ _____

The Liberty Bell

"It's not God or country, it's God and country!"
Ed Moore

Lesson Five
The Great National Deception
What Has Happened To Our Nation And Why

The Liberty Bell

Nobody knows when the Liberty Bell cracked. We do know that the original bell, cast in England, cracked the very first time the clapper struck it in 1753. It was immediately melted down and recast by two men by the now famous names of Pass and Stow. When the sound was found to be inferior, due to the addition of too much copper, the bell was immediately broken up and recast again. This is the bell that we are all familiar with today. During the Revolutionary War, the bell was hidden in the basement of the Zion Reformed Church in Allentown, Pennsylvania, in order to keep the British from recasting it as a cannon. In 1828, the bell was the object of court litigation because the maker of a new bell for the City of Philadelphia, John Wilbanks, refused to haul the old bell off. So there it sat.

In 1839, William Lloyd Garrison's anti-slavery publication, *The Liberator*, printed a poem entitled, *The Liberty Bell*. This was the first time that the now famous name is known to have been used in connection with the unwanted old relic. Sometime during all this, the bell developed a hairline crack. Nobody knows just when. Ironically however, it was not until February 22, 1846, as it rang in honor of George Washington's birthday, that the now famous zig-zag crack occurred. And, it was not until 1876, during America's first centennial birthday celebration, that the old bell finally became the revered and lasting symbol of freedom that it is today. Through all of this, one simple verse from the Bible, Leviticus 25:10, inscribed on both the original and recast bells, has born testimony to America's great purpose. It simply reads:

"Proclaim LIBERTY throughout all the Land
unto all the inhabitants thereof."

179

However, it is the symbolic *crack* that we want to concern ourselves with in this lesson. Just as this bell is inscribed with a Bible verse, so we must remember the Biblical roots of our nation's liberty. Just as the bell was abandoned, so we must not abandon America in her hour of spiritual need. And finally, just as a church provided protective custody of the Liberty Bell during the American Revolution, so likewise, America's churches must once again come to the defense of our nation's spiritual heritage. That brings us to the symbolism of the crack. Today, a war is raging to separate the United States from the moorings of her founding faith.

Defining The Crack

At the same time that our Executive and Legislative branches of government (the President and Congress) were reaffirming the spiritual heritage of our nation, (by officially sanctioning our national motto, our national anthem, and adding the words, *"Under God"* to our pledge, etc.) others were hatching a diabolical plan to use the third branch of government (the courts) as a vehicle to bypass the two elected branches in a sneak attack on our nation's spiritual heritage. The plan was to use the courts to silence the church, and then to euthenize God, religion and morality from all publicly sanctioned expressions, especially in our schools. By this means, a small minority of radical judges could use the court system to usurp and exert unconstitutional power in an effort to silence the church and intercept religion's future influence upon America. Thus, the same ban on religious influence that exists in communist countries, could be enforced upon America in the guise of preserving liberty.

This was not the first time that attempts were made to use the courts to attack religion in America. The only difference was that this time they had obtained a one-vote majority on the United States Supreme Court that would back up the rogue decrees of a few renegade judges. The result is that we have now raised a generation of Americans in our public schools that confuse freedom *of* religion with freedom *from* religion. The courts have been the exclusive vehicle for the implementation of this evil plan. Symbolically speaking, *this is the crack in the liberty bell*!

Unless this demonic assault on religion is countered by a head on counter-offensive by the Executive and Legislative (the elected) branches of our government, the illegitimate rulings will continue to destroy the moral fabric of our nation. The needed counter-assault will never materialize unless the church tears the gag from her mouth and defies all attempts to silence her. To this end we say, *"Rise up O men of God!"*

Let me state it again. The crack in our liberty is this: usurping judges have misused and abused their positions to neutralize the spiritual heritage of our nation. They have ignored our spiritual heritage and deceived us concerning religion's traditional place in America. Our presidents, our entire elected congress, and the whole of our society have cowed before this judicial tyranny. By one-vote margins, non-elected judges have neutralized the other branches of government to become tyrants of the nation. By disenfranchising morality and religion in public life, (something George Washington warned us about) this handful of wicked men has unraveled the spiritual fabric of our whole society. Chaos, immorality and lawlessness have been the result.

• Where we once had civility - crass vulgarity is now exalted.
• Where we once had decency and respect - frothing malcontents now burn our flag and belch forth their antichrist blasphemies.
• Where we once had purity - adultery, rape and sodomy exist.
• Where we once had Bible reading and prayer in our schools - we now have school gangs, mass murders, illicit sex, gang rapes, teenage pregnancy and rampant suicide.
• Where we once had statesmen, we now have self-seeking, morally depraved political hacks with little courage and less conviction. (Thank God there are exceptions!)

All of this has come upon us because we let illegitimate *"five to four"* decisions stand without the will to fight back. In my opinion, these usurping judges with their humanistic, Darwinian agenda, should be held in contempt of America! These men have proven the Bible maxim that: *"One sinner destroyeth much good."* (Ecclesiastes 9:18) In the case of the Supreme Court, we have seen that by a one-vote majority, a small group of judicial tyrants can destroy 400 years of godly heritage in a nation. Just yesterday on the news, I heard of the New Jersey Supreme Court handing down a ruling to force the New Jersey Legislature to honor homosexual *"rights"*. This kind of judicial usurpation and tyranny must be confronted and eradicated. Decent God-fearing Americans must unite and demand a constitutional redress of grievances. We must seek for rectification of these evils by an act of our publicly elected representatives in the Congress of the United States.

A Country Must Have Moral Law!

As we have seen from our first two lessons, our nation's Founding Fathers and Presidents alike, were clear that society had to have foundations in religious moral law. (See quotes by Washington on page 109; by Madison on page 112; by Adams on page 113; by Lincoln on page 114; by Roosevelt on page 115; by Eisenhower on page 120; etc. etc.) These men knew that without religion and morality, nothing could be considered *"wrong,"* and thus, every form of evil behavior would be protected and promulgated under the guise of *"liberty."* This is exactly what the Bible warns us about when it says: *"While they promise them liberty, they themselves are the servants of corruption."* (II Peter 2:19) Indeed, those who espouse that there can be no absolute rights and wrongs in a society's laws, actually use our sacred *"liberty, as a cloak of maliciousness"* (I Peter 2:16), to destroy the fabric of the nation. In so doing, these people are guilty of *"turning the grace of our God into lasciviousness."* (Jude 1:4)

This is the emerging problem in America today. Due to recent court rulings, evil is being protected as *"a constitutional right,"* while religion and morality are under court-sanctioned attack. If this is left unchecked, the escalating wickedness will eventually end with lawlessness in the streets, and the destruction of our nation. The Bible says: *"Righteousness exalteth a nation: but sin is a reproach to any people."* (Proverb 14:34) Let us throw off the reproach of this court-sanctioned sin. If we do not, then we may expect Divine judgment for dealing falsely with our God, just as John Winthrop warned from the decks of the *Arabella* nearly 400 years ago. The Bible is clear, *"The wicked shall be turned into hell, and all the nations that forget God."* (Psalm 9:17)

The Purpose Of Government

Government serves many purposes and has many legitimate functions. The Bible teaches us that God establishes nations and leaders in order to rule in the affairs of men. All governments are not good, but even evil governments serve a purpose. The truth of the matter is that we get the kind of government that we deserve. (A thought that I find frightening.) God is always responding to the consensus of the nations. If a nation honors God, He blesses it. If a nation forgets God's laws, He judges it by allowing its destruction or by allowing an oppressive government to come to power.

From the time of our nation's founding, to just after World War II, the United States enjoyed a government that based its laws upon the inherited Biblical concepts of good and evil. Our various levels of governments enforced these concepts of good and evil through various laws. Actually, this is one of the primary functions of government. The Bible says: *"For rulers are not a terror to good works, but to the evil."* (Romans 13:3)

However, when nations deny that there is an immutable foundation for moral behavior, how then can right and wrong be defined? More importantly, if government is powerless to define good and evil, how can government then fulfill its roll in promoting good and punishing evil? A lawless society is the inevitable result, and the destruction of the nation occurs from within. Soon, even presidents begin to flaunt lewd behavior, *"Just because I could."* This is exactly what President Hoover warned us about when he said:

> *"Our strength lies in spiritual concepts. It lies in public sensitivities to evil. Our greatest danger is not from invading armies. Our dangers are that we may commit suicide from within by complaisance with evil, or by public tolerance of scandalous behavior."*

This is the same thing that George Washington meant when he said:

> *"The propitious smiles of Heaven can never be expected on a nation that disregards the eternal rules of order and right, which heaven itself has ordained."*

Again, this is what Abraham Lincoln meant when he said:
"The only assurance of our nation's safety is to
lay our foundation in morality and religion."
The trouble is that we are not listening to nor honoring the God of our Founding Fathers any more. Instead, we have allowed a handful of old men in black robes to defile our Constitution with rulings that have totally disregarded 450 years of American history and 150 years of previously established court precedent. How did this occur and what can we do to counter it?

The Seduction of the Courts

There are several reasons that the anti-God, anti-morality forces tagged the courts as the most vulnerable vehicle to advance the hopes of their godless agenda. Consider:

1. Because the legislative and executive branches were moving in the direction of affirming instead of abandoning our spiritual heritage, any hope of making headway against religion there appeared fruitless. Inasmuch as these two branches of government have to answer to the people, it became doubly necessary to target the non-elected judicial branch to advance their agenda.

2. Because judges are, for the most part, appointed positions, it became much easier and cheaper to lobby for the appointment of lawyers who were in agreement with their agenda, than to vie in the never-ending and very expensive struggle of trying to elect and control members of the other branches.

3. Because judicial appointees are not under as much public and legislative scrutiny as presidential and congressional candidates, it was easy to have a lawyer appointed whose views on yet unforeseen contests were not known before the fact. In effect, it became easy to stack the deck in anticipation of the barrage of attacks that soon followed.

4. Because judges are, for the most part, appointed for life, there could be no repercussions from an angry electorate to terminate their stay in office or reverse their radical judicial decrees. Therefore, once in place, and once the onslaught began, there would be no short-term recourse to stop the judicial tyranny.

5. Because it would take years for the opposition to realize what had happened and many more years to replace such judges with good ones, their judicial decrees would be imposed and institutionalized before the opposition could regain their footing. By then, new "*court precedents*" would have been firmly established, and, barring an all out American revolt, these would be impossible to reverse.

This is what happened, and to date it has succeeded. We are now at the crossroads of either capitulating to the judicial takeover of America, or finding both the will and the leadership to retake our nation.

Established Historic Precedents

In legal terms, an established "*precedent*" where court rulings are concerned, is a decision that *has* been made and then grows stronger as it withstands legal challenges over the ensuing years. Over time, these precedents have a trickling down effect, becoming the basis for all future decisions and so on.

In the first 100 years of our nation's history, literally no one questioned the validity of Christian morality or the Bible as the basis for the laws of our land. In 1892, The United States Supreme Court acknowledged this fact stating:

> "*Because of a general recognition of this truth, the question has seldom been presented to the courts.*"

However, when challenges to the status quo did come, case law universally supported the precedent of protecting religion and its influence within the public domain. While it is impossible in a book this size to present the volume of overwhelming evidence, allow me to quote from one Supreme Court opinion that faithfully represents the state of American legal opinion for the entirety of our nation's first 150 years.

The U. S. Supreme Court Affirms Our Christian Heritage

In the 1892 case of *Church of the Holy Trinity v. United States*, the matter of our nation's Christian heritage was meticulously documented and reaffirmed by the high court. In my opinion, this is one of the grandest opinions ever articulated by the United States Supreme Court. In handing down the decision, the Court undergirded its opinion by affirming the historically established practice of basing America's moral laws on Biblical, Christian principles. In consideration of time and space, I will quote excerpts from the sixteen-page opinion along with running commentary that faithfully summarizes the gaps. The Court said:

> *"This is a religious people. This is historically true.*
> *From the discovery of this continent, to this present*
> *hour, there is a single voice making this affirmation.*

The opinion then quotes from the commission to Columbus; from the first colonial grant to Sir Walter Raleigh, 1584; from the first charter of Virginia, 1606 and subsequent charters of 1609 and 1611; from the Mayflower Compact, 1620; from the fundamental orders of Connecticut, 1638; and from the charter issued by William Penn to the province of Pennsylvania, 1701. Each and all of these were legal and binding originating documents that invoked the name of God and the Christian faith as part of their authorization. The Supreme Court opinion then progresses to the time of our nation's founding days stating:

> *"Coming nearer to the present time, the*
> *Declaration of Independence recognizes the presence*
> *of the Divine in human affairs in these words,*
>> *'We hold these truths to be self*
>> *evident, that all men are created equal,*
>> *that they are endowed by their Creator*
>> *with certain unalienable rights. . .',*
>> *'. . . appealing to the Supreme Judge*
>> *of the world for the rectitude of our*
>> *intentions. . .'*
>> *'And for the support of this*
>> *declaration, and with firm reliance on*
>> *the protection of Divine Providence. . .'*

The opinion then goes on citing example after example, quoting from the state constitutions of the 44 states then in the Union. The opinion then concludes:

> *"There is no dissonance in these declarations.*
> *There is a universal language pervading them all,*
> *having one meaning; they affirm and reaffirm that this*

is a religious nation. These are not individual sayings,
declarations of private persons; they are organic
utterances; they speak the voice of the entire people."

The word "organic," when used in the legal sense, means that the thing referred to is derived from official bodies representing official policy. This is important. The U. S. Supreme Court then quotes two previous decisions by the Supreme Courts of Pennsylvania and New York respectively, and then refers to a previous decision by the Supreme Court made some 48 years earlier. We continue quoting:

"We find that in 'Updegraph v. The Commonwealth',
[1824] it was decided that,

> *'Christianity, general Christianity, is,*
> *and always has been, a part of common*
> *law. . . not Christianity with an*
> *established church. . . but Christianity*
> *with liberty of conscience to all men.'*

And in 'The People v. Ruggles', [1811] Chancellor
Kent, the great commentator on American law,
speaking as Chief Justice of the state of New York,
said:

> *'The people of this state, in common*
> *with the people of this country, profess*
> *the general doctrines of Christianity, as*
> *the rule of their faith and practice. . . We*
> *are a Christian people, and the morality*
> *of the country is deeply engrafted upon*
> *Christianity, and not upon the doctrines*
> *or worship of those imposters.'*

And in the famous [1844, U.S. Supreme Court] case
of 'Vidal v. Girard's Executors', this court observed:

> *'These and many other matters which*
> *might be noticed, add to the volume of*
> *unofficial declarations to the mass of*
> *organic utterances that this is a Christian*
> *nation.'"*

Thus, by this ruling, the United States Supreme Court rightfully confirmed 400 years of undeniable evidence that the United States was, and always had been a Christian nation, and that its laws were based upon Christian common law. This is how things stood with the courts deep into the middle of the twentieth century.

Our Founding Congress

The original Continental Congress, which gave birth to our American Independence, and the subsequently elected Constitutional Congress of the United States have both issued the same conclusions to those so eloquently expressed in the previous Supreme Court ruling.

For instance, in 1777, during the crises of the American Revolution, Bibles became scarce. In order to rectify this dilemma, Congress adopted a report by a special committee to authorize the purchase of 20,000 Bibles from overseas to meet the demand. The committee reported:

> *"That the use of the Bible is so universal, and its importance so great. . . your committee recommends that Congress will order the Committee of Commerce to import 20,000 Bibles from Holland, Scotland or elsewhere, into different parts of the States of the Union."*

In 1781, Congress approved a petition from Robert Aitkin, publisher of *The Pennsylvania Magazine*, to authorize *"a neat edition of the Holy Scriptures to be used in public schools"*. This Bible, (the first to be printed in the United States) became known as *"The Bible of the Revolution"* and is one of the rarest books in the world today. In authorizing the printing, Congress said:

> *"Whereupon, Resolved. . . That the United States in Congress Assembled. . . recommend this edition of the Bible to the inhabitants of the United States, and*

hereby authorize to publish this recommendation in the manner he shall think proper."

As demonstrated by the above examples, our Founding Fathers harbored no hostilities toward religion nor hesitated to *officially* encourage the printing and dissemination of the Bible in our land.

America Beheld As A Christian Nation

After our new Constitution and Bill of Rights were adopted, Christianity's influence upon the land continued to be honored and cherished. America was seen as a glorious example of the virtue and happiness that is afforded to a Christian nation. When Alexis de Tocqueville visited the United States in the early 1830's, he published what he observed in a book entitled, *Democracy in America*. To this day, it remains a powerful snapshot of what America was like forty to fifty years after the Constitution was approved. Allow me to present a few revealing quotes. He wrote:

> *"There is no country in the whole world in which the Christian religion retains a greater influence over the souls of men than in America and there can be no better proof of its utility, and of its conformity to human nature, than that its influence is most powerfully felt over the most enlightened and free nation on earth."*

Concerning the education of children in the country he observed that, *"Almost all education is left to the clergy."* He further revealed in these observations that:

> *"The Americans combine the notions of Christianity and of liberty so intimately in their minds, that it is impossible to make them conceive one without the other."*

And again,

> *"In the United States, if a political character attacks a sect, (a denomination) this may not prevent even the partisans of that sect, from supporting him; but if he attacks all sects together, (Christianity in general) everyone abandons him and he remains alone."*

Today however, there is a concerted effort to stop Christianity's historic sway over the laws of our land.

Corroborating Congressional Conclusions

When the challenges of the ungodly did finally begin to occur, not only did the courts consistently rule *against* them, Congress itself passed judgement on the larger question of whether or not the United States was indeed a Christian nation. In the mid 1850's, having failed in the courts, the opponents of religion in America petitioned Congress to remove Chaplains from the halls of Congress and from the military. Both the House and Senate considered the matter and both issued statements. On January 19,1853 the Committee in the House of Representatives issued its recommendation stating:

> *"We are a Christian people. . . and in a land thus universally Christian, what is to be expected, what desired, but that we shall pay a due regard to Christianity?"*

In addressing the meaning of the first amendment, which prohibits Congress from acting in the *"establishment of religion, nor prohibiting the free exercise thereof. . . "* The report continued:

> *"The whole view of the petitioners seems founded upon mistaken conceptions of the meaning of the Constitution. . . They [our Forefathers] intended, by this amendment, to prohibit 'an established of religion' such as the English Church presented, or anything like it. But, they had no fear or jealousy of religion itself, nor did they wish to see us an irreligious people. . . They did not intend to spread over all the public authorities and the whole public action of the nation the dead and revolting spectacle of atheistic apathy."*

A little over a year later, on March 27, the Senate Committee on the Judiciary issued its conclusion stating:

> *"Had the people, during the Revolution, had a suspicion of any attempt to war against Christianity, that Revolution would have been strangled in its cradle."*

The Senate report went on to state:

> *"It [Christianity] must be considered the*

foundation on which the whole structure rests. Laws will not have permanence or power without the sanction of religious sentiment, without a firm belief that there is a power above us that will reward our virtues and punish our vices. In this age, there can be no substitute for Christianity; that, in its general principles, is the great conservative element in which we must rely for purity and permanence of free institutions. That was the religion of the founders of the republic, and they expected it to remain the religion of their descendants."

Today's Godless Mess

After reading the foregoing lessons containing so much evidence about our Christian heritage, you may be asking, *"Since all of this is true, how did we get into the mess that our country finds itself in today?"* I will briefly describe what happened and what must be done to correct the situation.

The Great Deception Begins

The crack in our American heritage started when judges began to abuse the separation of powers as prescribed in the Constitution. Instead of issuing opinions on questions put before it, the court itself began to usurp the powers reserved exclusively to the other two branches of government. Judges have no right to legislate by decree because they are not directly elected by the people. Nevertheless, signs of the opportunity for judicial abuse began to appear early on in our nation's history.

In the modern context, this abuse of power first exerted itself when the high court denied 150 years of established precedents, to introduce a new doctrine that had *never* before been tolerated. I am speaking of the myth promulgated under the non-constitutional phrase, *"the separation of church and state"*. I call this a myth, because none, not one, of our founding documents uses the term! It would be better to call this doctrine *"a deception"* because its promoters have deceived Americans by implying that this phrase has its roots in the

Constitution, the Bill of Rights, or in the mass of our nation's supporting organic utterances. It does not! In fact the origin of the phrase is from a non-organic (unofficial, personal utterance) of just one man, and even that it is taken totally out of context and misused! Instead of safeguarding the church from government intrusion and control, the new court redefined the phrase as a new battle cry *against* religion and morality in America.

All Of Our Christian History Erased
By A Single, One-Vote Margin!

In 1947, in the case known as *Everson v. The Board of Education*, the greatest legal hijacking in history took place. In this case, the court shocked the legal world when it ignored all historic precedent and reinterpreted the First Amendment, (part of the original Bill of Rights), by using the Fourteenth Amendment, (part of package of four post-civil war amendments addressing slavery issues). This application was never intended and had *never, ever* before been made in the entire 77 year history of the latter amendment! In short, this was a cheap, dishonest legal maneuver unworthy of even the slimiest of lawyers. In effect, the high court created a new power for itself; a power through which it began reinterpreting the First Amendment contrary to the original intent of our Founding Fathers and 150 years of firmly established court precedents! By using this new and bogus interpretation, even our Founding Fathers were themselves indicted of violating the very Constitution that they had written. This is insanity! *And it all came about by a one-vote margin!*

It was also in this ruling that the high court first used the so-called *"wall of separation"* phrase. By doing this they began laying the groundwork to silence the one and only institution that they feared, the church. And this was just the beginning!

The Buzzword Trickles Down

As a result of this power-grabbing, heritage-raping, five to four decision, the liberal legal system went crazy attacking every vestige of Christian influence in the land. The so-called *"Wall of Separation"* term became so popular that by 1958 one ruling lamented,

> *"Much has been written in recent years concerning Thomas Jefferson's reference in 1802 to 'a wall of separation between church and state'. . . Jefferson's figure of speech has received so much attention that one would almost think at times that it is to be found somewhere in our Constitution."*
>
> Baer v. Kolmorgen, 1958

The Warren Court, became so rampant and embarrassing in its decisions that President Eisenhower, who had nominated Earl Warren as Chief Justice of the Supreme Court, said: *"Nominating Warren to the Chief Justice seat was the biggest *@#!!-fool mistake I ever made."* (expletive deleted) Liberals began adoringly referring to Warren as *"The Superchief"* because of how much of their agenda he was able to *railroad* through the Supreme Court. Here are just a few of the infamous decisions that the Warren court handed down.

Prayer and Bible Reading
Banned From Public Education

Having laid the groundwork for this *"new precedent,"* the humanistic enemies of God were now ready to strike at the very heart of religion in America. Once the trickling down effect was firmly established, they moved with rapid fury to ravage the heritage of our nation by accepting cases which could be used as vehicles to make unprecedented rulings, which they forced down the throats of Americans by judicial decrees. Their first and most important goal was to eradicate every form of religious expression from public education.

In the 1962 case of *Engel v. Vitale*, the high court shocked the nation by declaring voluntary prayer in public schools *"unconstitutional"*. In making this ruling, the court did not cite a single precedent to support its decision. This is because there was not a single historical case that they could use to support it!

This decision was quickly followed by the 1963 case of *Abington v. Schempp*, in which 150 years of Bible reading in public schools was also declared to be *"unconstitutional"*. America reeled in disbelief under the rulings while the White House and Congress both sat passively by.

Pandora's Box Is Opened

After the two-edged sword of these two initial rulings was issued, nothing sacred was spared as godless lawyers at every level initiated lawsuits directed at every other form of public religious expression in America. As a result, a Pandora's box was opened without restraint. Every evil imaginable came pouring into the clean water of our society. Anti-pornography laws were declared a violation of free speech. Abortion was ruled to be the constitutional right of every woman, and today, homosexual marriages are being forced upon our nation through godless court decrees. Enough! All this must stop! It is time for God-fearing Americans to stand up against this insanity.

The Bible says: *"If the foundations be destroyed, what can the righteous do?"* (Psalm 11:3) It also says, *"When the wicked beareth rule, the people mourn."* (Proverbs 29:2) These two verses pretty much sum up what happened under the Warren Court, and to a great extent, under the Burger Court as well. The wicked have literally destroyed the Christian foundations of our country, and our children are mourning as a result.

The Verdict Is Coming In

Concerning the courts controversial rulings, Earl Warren said, *"We may not know the whole story in our lifetime."* This is one of the few things that Warren said that I could agree with. The destructive repercussions of the Supreme Court's actions upon our children and the moral fabric of our nation cannot possibly be assessed. However, as the returns continue to come in, they are becoming increasingly more dismal. Since the Supreme Court banned prayer and Bible reading in our public schools, consider the results:

• Divorce rates have more than doubled.

• Unwed girls giving birth has increased two and a half times.

• Sexually transmitted diseases have quadrupled.

• Violent crime has doubled itself three times over.

To continue to press the point by adding more facts and figures is unnecessary. Americans have lived through the moral rape of our nation and they can see the score. They know that they have been lied to and hoodwinked. Former Congresswoman, Katherine Harris (R-Florida) has called the separation of church and state *"a lie,"* and she is not alone. In fact, a recent Pew Forum survey indicates that 67% of all Americans believe that the United States was founded as a Christian nation. Everywhere I go, I see people who are hungry for a return to decency. As a result of the latest election, over half of our states have now rallied to reaffirm that marriage is between one man and one woman. We are finally discovering that *we the people*, can fight back!

One Man Stands Up Against Judicial Tyranny

Almost all Americans are familiar with the celebrated case in which Alabama Chief Justice Roy Moore refused to remove the Ten Commandments from the Alabama capitol building, and in so doing openly defied federal court tyranny. Moore's resulting political martyrdom refocused America's attention on the reality of judicial tyranny and has re-

Photo courtesy of Baptist Press

energized Christian involvement in the political spectrum. While the final chapter has not yet been written on Judge Moore's future, he stands as an inspiring example of genuine courage and true patriotism.

Of course, the Supreme Court refused to hear the case on appeal, in spite of the hypocritical fact that the Ten Commandments are all over the Supreme Court building in

Washington D.C. Maybe this is why the court whimped out on the opportunity to review the case. I offer this little jingle of a poem to honor Judge Moore, and to remind Americans that the influence of his valiant stand is yet to be fully appreciated and felt.

The Value of Courage
He who is courageous,
Will find himself contagious.
And he, who takes a valiant stand,
Will inspire many a man.

The Elected Branches Of Government Must
Re-exert Themselves Against Judicial Tyranny.

The reason that judicial tyranny is running amuck is because the elected representatives of the people have not stood up against the court's usurpation of powers. Earlier in our nation's history this was not the case. In 1832, when the Supreme Court ordered President Andrew Jackson to implement certain court orders, "Old Hickory" simply replied, "*[The Chief Justice] made his decision, now let him enforce it.*" Jackson explained his objections to Congress stating:

> "*Each public officer who takes the oath to support the Constitution, swears that he will support it as he understands it, and not as it is understood by others. . . The opinion of the judges has no more authority over the Congress than the opinion of Congress has over the judges, and on that point, the President is independent of both. The authority of the Supreme Court must not, therefore, be permitted to control the Congress or the Executive.*"   (July 10, 1832)

President Jackson properly understood that for the executive branch to bow down to a handful of non-elected judges would mean abandoning the separation of powers between the branches of government.

James Madison, "The *Father of the Constitution*", concurred on this point, having stated earlier:

"Nothing has yet been offered to invalidate the doctrine that the meaning of the Constitution may as well be ascertained by the legislature as by the judicial authority."

President Abraham Lincoln made it very clear that judicial supremacy would lead to thwarting the rule of the people. In his first Inaugural Address, Lincoln stated:

"I do not forget the position of some that constitutional questions are to be decided by the Supreme Court. . . At the same time, the candid citizen must confess that if the policy of the government upon vital questions affecting the whole people is to be irrevocably fixed by decisions of the Supreme Court, the instant they are made. . . the people will have ceased to be their own rulers, having. . . resigned their government into the hands of that eminent tribunal."

The solution is for the people to exercise their God-given right to self-determination through their *elected* branches of government. The people must demand that their elected leaders re-exert the will of the people against social engineering by those practicing judicial tyranny. We must pray and ask God to raise up leaders that will have the moral courage to lead our country in repudiating those decisions that have robbed us of our moral foundations. Since everything rises and falls upon leadership, and since it is God who ultimately sets up and removes such leaders, we as a people must *first* return to God in our hearts. Only then will He raise up such a leader or leaders to deliver us from the bondage of the ungodly. We see this pattern confirmed again and again in the Holy Scriptures. If we will return to God, He *will* come to our aid!

The Obvious Question

In light of all that we have presented, one obvious question remains to be answered. *"Can the crack in the Liberty Bell be repaired?"* The answer is that only God can repair some things, and thankfully, nothing is too hard for God! Even now I see some very encouraging signs.

Those who destroy nations, have never dealt with a nation quite like the United States. There is one thing that they have forgotten, if they ever knew it; and that is the fact that America is *still* a Christian nation! Yes, there is a great deal of sin in our land. Yes, Hollywood is pouring out unbelievable filth as never before. And yes, our internal enemies have gained a temporary advantage through the courts. Yet, deep within the American soul is a heart that knows where we came from, and that we need to return to the God of our fathers.

Everywhere I go, I see the people of our country openly expressing a need to pray for America. We are again looking in the right direction. . . we are looking up! The job of *Prayer Force One* is to fan these flickering flames of potential revival. We must collect and unite the embers wherever they burn into one mighty fire of national renewal. I am asking every red-blooded, God-fearing American to help us in this hour. May God, Himself cause the Liberty Bell to once again ring out with the clarion call of holy freedom!

Lesson Five: Open Book Quiz
(See how much you can remember. Answers begin on page 244)

1. What Bible verse is printed on the Liberty Bell? _____

2. Complete this Bible verse from Proverbs 14:34 *"Righteousness exalteth _____ but sin is a reproach to any_____."*

3. Complete this Bible verse from Psalm 9:17 *"The wicked shall be turned into hell, and all the nations that _____."*

4. Which of our presidents said: *"The only assurance of our nation's safety is to lay our foundation in morality and religion."* _____
_____

5. Fill in the blanks of this statement by President Hoover. *"Our strength lies in _____concepts. It lies in public sensitivities to _____. Our greatest danger is not from invading armies. Our dangers are that we may commit suicide from within by complaisance with evil, or by _____ tolerance of scandalous behavior."*

6. Complete this 1844 Supreme Court quote. *"These and many other matters which might be noticed, add to the volume of unofficial declarations to the mass of organic utterances that this is _____
_____."*

7. In 1777, during the Revolutionary War, how many Bibles did the Continental Congress order to be imported to America? _____

8. On January 19,1853, the U.S. House of Representatives stated: *"We are a _____People, and in a land thus universally _____, what is to be expected, what desired, but that we shall pay a due regard to _____?"*

9. On March 27, the Senate Committee on the Judiciary issued this statement: *"Had the people, during the Revolution, had a suspicion of any attempt to _____ against Christianity, that Revolution would have been strangled in its _____."*

10. In 1947, in the case known as *Everson v. The Board of Education*, the Supreme Court nullified 150 years of established court precedents of recognizing Christianity by a _____-vote margin.

11. Which U.S. President said: *"Nominating Warren to the Chief Justice seat was the biggest *@#!!-fool mistake I ever made."* (expletive deleted) _____

"Blessed is the nation whose God is the LORD."
Psalm 33:12

Lesson Six
"Blessed Is The Nation"
Keeping Faith With The God Of Our Fathers

The Blessings and Dangers of Pluralism

America enjoys freedom of worship, and no one that I've talked to wants to see that change. Freedom of religion is one of the great concepts that Christian America has championed and bequeathed to the world. One of the reasons that this is so, is because Christians themselves have so often been the victim of intolerant religious and political persecution. In founding our nation, our Christian forefathers understood that to enjoy freedom from persecution, there must be freedom for all to worship as they pleased. This is one of the great supporting tenets of the American concept of freedom. This is also one of the reasons why America has difficulty exporting freedom to religiously intolerant nations.

However, for all the blessings that freedom of religion affords the citizens of a nation, there are also inherent dangers that go along with this freedom. These dangers must be recognized and understood. The most serious of these dangers is that the enemies of God endeavor to enforce the concept that freedom *of* religion means freedom *from* religion in all things public. When this happens, the foundations for all public morality are destroyed. The result is that ungodliness is protected while the ability to enforce decency is effectively hobbled. I think Ronald Reagan said it best when he stated:

> *"From the early days of the colonies, prayer in school was practiced and revered as an important tradition. Indeed, for nearly two hundred years of our nation's history, it was considered a natural expression*

201

of our religious freedom. But in 1962 the Supreme Court handed down a controversial decision prohibiting prayer in public schools.

Sometimes I can't help but feel the First Amendment is being turned on its head. Because, you ask yourselves: Can it really be true that the First Amendment can permit Nazis and Klu Klux Klansmen to march on public property, advocate the extermination of people of the Jewish faith and the subjugation of blacks, while the same amendment forbids our children from saying a prayer in school?"

("*Prayer In Public Schools*" radio address,
Camp David, Maryland, February 25, 1984)

President Reagan again addressed this misconception head on when he said:

"I believe that schoolchildren deserve the same right to pray that's enjoyed by the Congress and chaplains and troops in our armed services. The motto on our coinage reads, 'In God We Trust.' No one must ever be forced or pressured to take part in any religious exercise, but neither should the government forbid religious practice. The <u>public</u> expression of prayer of our faith in God is a fundamental part of our American heritage and a privilege which should not be excluded from our schools.

("*Domestic Social Issues*" radio address,
Camp David, Maryland, January 22, 1983)

As a result of this erroneous "*separation*" mentality, an environment of hostility toward religion actually emerges. Let me illustrate. When the Supreme Court broke faith with our past and ruled against school prayer and Bible reading, children who continued to pray and read their Bibles actually became targets of persecution. For instance:

• In Omaha, Nebraska a ten-year-old student was told by school authorities that it was against the law to read or even open his Bible during free time at school.

• In 1987 students in Alaska were told that they could no longer use the word *Christmas* at school because it had the word Christ in it.
• In Colorado Springs, Colorado, a music teacher stopped leading her class in the singing of Christmas carols because of accusations of *violating* the Constitution.

These are not just isolated cases. Instead, they are indicative of the kind of hostile environment that develops when society becomes intolerant to public expressions of faith. As a result, we are now living in a society where God is not venerated as having any authority over our laws. Consequently, our nation is now in danger of totally disregarding the God of our fathers and of the religious precepts upon which our historic laws are based. An atheistic environment of publicly protected vulgarity is now the result, and if not checked, will continue to eat at our national soul until the nation is destroyed from within.

It is with this danger, the danger of forgetting God, that we want to concern ourselves with in this lesson. We as Americans are now faced with a literal war over the soul of our nation. If we capitulate to the forces of darkness and immorality, we will follow in the fate of all other nations that forget God.

Americans Themselves Must Decide

If we are a nation that believes its motto, "*In God We Trust,*" we must first recognize who God is. Is He the God of our Founding Fathers? Is He the God of the Bible? Is He the God of Abraham, Isaac and Jacob? Is He the God and Father of our LORD Jesus Christ? Or, is He just a humanistic conglomeration of the smorgasbord of gods that people may choose to worship? While I understand perfectly well that any citizen can worship any god they choose, does this mean that we must reject the Christian foundations upon which our historic laws are based? Does this mean, contrary to what our Founding Fathers have said, that we must reject religious precepts as the foundations of our moral laws? In the five centuries of life in America, not one generation of Americans thought so until now!

Today, we are being told that we must change; yea, a godless agenda is being forced down our throats in the guise of liberty. We are being told that the LORD God who shed his grace upon America must move over because of a new humanistic interpretation of the Constitution, which allows for *no* public acknowledgment of God or His laws. This is nonsense. I believe that there is a great praying majority of Americans that desire the United States to once again embrace the God of our fathers. And it is just here, in the heart of all Americans, that this battle will be won or lost. If we, as a people, once again affirm our faith and trust in God, no court on earth will prevail against us, for our God will stand beside us.

> # *"Blessed is the nation whose God is the LORD."*
> # Psalm 33:12

The Bible faithfully promises: *"Blessed is the nation whose God is the LORD."* (Psalm 33:12) Again, I quote Abraham Lincoln's strong acknowledgment of this truth when he said:

"It is the <u>duty</u> of nations as well as men, to own their dependence upon the overruling power of God and to recognize the sublime truth announced in the Holy Scriptures and proven by all history, that those nations only are blessed whose God is the LORD."

Notice that President Abraham Lincoln specifically acknowledged that it was the *duty* of nations to own their dependence upon the LORD God of the Bible.

"Who Is The LORD That I Should Obey Him?"

When the Bible says, *"Blessed is the nation whose God is the LORD,"* just who is it talking about? Who is this *"LORD"*? Strangely enough, this is the very same question that Pharaoh defiantly asked when Moses, speaking in the name of the LORD, said: *"Let My people go!"* Pharaoh hotly retorted to Moses by asking, *"Who is the LORD, that I should obey his voice?"* (Exodus 5:2) This is the question that America must also answer if we are to continue to be blessed by God. Pharaoh mocked and rejected the LORD God, and this led to his death, and also to the destruction of his nation.

"The LORD, He Is The God!"
In I Kings 18, the false prophets of Baal were challenged by the prophet, Elijah, to prove just who the true and living God was. When the LORD answered by fire, the people themselves issued the verdict by crying out, *"The LORD, he is the God, the LORD, he is the God!"* (I Kings 18:39) Notice that the term "God" is a generic term for deity, while the term "LORD" is the specific name of the God of the Bible. We, as a nation, must decide in our collective heart if we also believe that the LORD is the one true and living God.

Choose Ye this Day
When Joshua led the children of Israel into Canaan, he challenged them to reaffirm their faith in the LORD. He said:

> *"Now therefore fear the LORD, and serve Him in sincerity and in truth: and put away the gods which your fathers served on the other side of the flood, and in Egypt; and serve ye the LORD. And if it seem evil unto you to serve the LORD, choose you this day whom ye will serve; whether the gods your fathers served that were on the other side of the flood, or the gods of the Amorites, in whose land ye dwell: but as for me and my house, we will serve the LORD.*
>
> *And the people answered and said, God forbid that we should forsake the LORD, to serve other gods: For the LORD our God, He it is that brought us up and our fathers out of the land of Egypt, from the house of bondage. . .therefore will we also serve the LORD; for he is our God."* (Joshua 24:14-18)

Today, we, like the children of Israel, must decide whether or not the God we trust is the God of our fathers, or whether He is just some nameless, generic concept referred to as God. We must decide if we believe that *"the LORD"* is the one who has blessed America, and whether or not we will continue to obey His voice.

The Consensus Of The Nation

Now, we understand that we cannot do this by a Presidential decree, or by some act of Congress. Instead, each and every one of us must make this decision in our hearts. We answer this question when we decide to embrace and defend the Christian heritage handed down to us by our Forefathers. This in turn is reflected in how we vote. At this very moment, I sit aboard *Prayer Force One,* writing this lesson. It is Election Day, November 6, 2006. The polls will close in about one hour. Since our church is used as a polling place, and since *Prayer Force One* sits just outside our church, I have watched as over three hundred and fifty of my neighbors have come to vote. As each one votes, God, Himself is taking note. He is tallying votes that no voting machine will ever be able to count. In a sense, God is counting the ballots of our hearts. Collectively, this forms what may be referred to as, *"the consensus of the nation."* It is reflected in our prayers, and in the way we live. If our hearts reflect a desire to embrace Godly principles, God continues to bless us. If, on the other hand, we embrace wickedness, God responds by withdrawing His blessings on our country. It is as simple as that.

This is what President Ronald Reagan was referring to when he said:

> *"Sometimes it seems we've strayed . . . from our convictions that standards of right and wrong do exist and must be lived up to. God, the source of our knowledge, has been expelled from the classroom. He gives us His greatest blessing, life, and yet many would condone the taking of innocent life. We expect Him to protect us in crises, but turn away from Him too often in our day-to-day living. I wonder if He isn't waiting for us to wake up."*

In this same context, Benjamin Franklin's words to the Continental Congress bear repeating:

> *"To that kind Providence we owe this happy opportunity . . . And have we now forgotten that*

*powerful Friend? Or do we imagine that we no longer
need His assistance?"*

Yes, by every thought and deed, as well as by every vote we
make on Election Day, we are casting a ballot as to whether or not
we will continue to honor the LORD God of our fathers.

Jesus Christ Is The LORD

Let me be more specific by presenting what the God of our Fathers
said about Himself. In Isaiah 43:11 God said:

*"I, even I, am the LORD; and beside me there is
no Savior."*

Again, in Isaiah, 44:6 we read:

*"Thus saith the LORD the King of Israel, and his
Redeemer the LORD of hosts; I am the first, and I am
the last; and beside me there is no God."*

In these two Old Testament scriptures, we find references to the
LORD, who is called both Savior and Redeemer. However, in the
New Testament book of Revelation, this Savior, this Redeemer, is
revealed as Christ Jesus the LORD, who is clearly called, *"the first
and the last"*. The Bible says:

*"I am Alpha and Omega, the beginning and the
ending, saith the LORD, which is, and which was,
and which is to come, the Almighty. . . Fear not; I am
the first and the last: I am he that liveth, and was
dead; and, behold, I am alive for evermore."*

(Revelation 1:8,17&18)

Here we are given to understand that the LORD of the Old
Testament is the crucified and risen Son of God who came down to
die for us in the New Testament. He is one and the same. This is why
he is called the LORD Jesus Christ.

The LORD Of Christmas

When the angels announced the birth of Christ at the first
Christmas, they confirmed that His birth was an event foretold in the
Old Testament book of Isaiah, where it was written:

"Therefore the LORD himself shall give you a sign;

Behold, a virgin shall conceive, and bear a son, and
shall call his name Immanuel"   (Isaiah 7:14)

This name, *Immanuel*, is very important for it means, "*God with us.*" The angel of the LORD quoted this Old Testament verse when he announces the birth of Jesus Christ. Notice what the angel said to Joseph in Matthew 1:20-23:

"The angel of the LORD appeared unto him in a dream, saying, Joseph, thou son of David, fear not to take unto thee Mary thy wife: for that which is conceived in her is of the Holy Ghost.

And she shall bring forth a son, and thou shalt call his name JESUS, (which means Savior) *for He shall save His people from their sins.*

Now all this was done, that it might be fulfilled which was spoken of the LORD by the prophet, saying,

Behold, a virgin shall be with child, and shall bring forth a son, and they shall call his name Emmanuel, which being interpreted is, God with us."

This was the faith of our fathers. We have already seen how

important President Franklin Delano Roosevelt considered the message of Christmas to be to our democracy. We again quote his words from October 28, 1944:

" *'Peace on earth, good will toward men' - democracy <u>must</u> cling to that message. For it is my deep conviction that <u>democracy cannot live without that true religion</u> which gives a nation a sense of justice and moral purpose."*

While Roosevelt believed in religious liberty as much as any man, there is no pluralistic apology reflected in this statement.

Listen also to the words of Harry Truman as he lit the national Christmas tree in December of 1950:

"At this time, we should renew our faith in God. <u>We celebrate the hour in which God came to man</u>. It is fitting that we should turn to Him. . . But there are

many others who are away from their homes and their loved ones on this day. Thousands of our boys are on the cold and dreary battlefield of Korea. But all of us, at home, at war, wherever we may be, are within reach of God's love and power. We can all pray. We should all pray."

How is it that today, preferring Christ, Christmas and the Christian religion are no longer considered American? We must reject the notion that to be an American we must renounce the faith of our Founding Fathers!

"I Will Bless Them That Bless Thee."

When the LORD God revealed His plan to bless *all* the nations of the earth through Abraham, He was referring specifically to Jesus Christ. In Galatians 3:16 the Apostle Paul wrote to clarify this point. He wrote:

"Now to Abraham and his seed were the promises made. He saith not, 'And to thy seeds', as of many; but as of one, 'And to thy seed', which is Christ."

In fact, the covenant blessing that God gave to Abraham was, in fact, the gospel of Jesus Christ, which was to come *through* him. Notice how the Bible confirms this in Galatians 3:8:

"And the Scripture, foreseeing that God would justify the heathen through faith, preached before the gospel unto Abraham, saying, 'In thee shall all nations be blessed."

Now along with this "Messianic" prophecy concerning the Savior, God also gave a promise to bless or curse others, based on how they treated Abraham and this promised seed. (Remember, that the promised seed is the promised Son of God!) God promised that:

"I will bless them that bless thee, and curse him that curseth thee: and in thee shall all families of the earth be blessed." (Genesis 12:3)

Because of this blessing/curse pact that God had with Abraham, he blessed and cursed those who would hurt Israel so long as Christ was carried in her matron womb. When Christ did eventually come, God continued to bless or curse nations in relation to how they blessed or cursed the Promised One, Jesus Christ. Israel, itself, found out that even she could get on the wrong side of the blessing/curse pact. Jesus told them,

> *"O Jerusalem, Jerusalem, thou that killest the prophets, and stonest them which are sent unto thee, how often would I have gathered thy children together, even as a hen gathereth her chickens under her wings, and ye would not! Behold, your house is left unto you desolate. For I say unto you, Ye shall not see me henceforth, till ye shall say, Blessed is he that cometh in the name of the LORD."* (Matthew 23:37-39)

America has been so richly blessed because of her faith in Jesus Christ. But if we forsake Him, God will not hesitate to punish us as well. In the Holy Scriptures, the Gentile nations are warned:

> *"For if God spared not the natural branches,* (Israel) *take heed lest he also spare not thee."*
>
> (Romans 11:20)

God is not through with the nation of Israel. The same scripture that tells us why they have had so much suffering, also goes on to foretell of a time, not too distant, when Israel will once again acknowledge the LORD Jesus Christ. (See Romans 11:15 as well as Zechariah, 12:10 and Hosea 5:15, etc.)

"Kiss the Son Lest He Be Angry"

The second Psalm is written to the kings and judges of the earth. It first foretells of the coming of the Son of God, saying, *"Thou art my Son, this day have I begotten thee."* (Compare Psalm 2:7 with Matthew 3:17, Acts 13:33 and Hebrews 1:5) Later in this same Psalm, King David warns the leaders of the earth to: *"Kiss the Son lest he be angry, and ye perish from the way, when his wrath is kindled but a little."* Here we again see that the LORD God of the Old Testament is the LORD God of the New Testament. This is why so many of our good leaders refer to America's Judeo-Christian heritage, for it is evident that we have *none other!*

"None Other Name Under Heaven"

With the last two words of the last paragraph in mind, notice what the Bible says about the name of Jesus Christ. In Acts 4:12, the two words, *"none other"* refer to the name of Jesus Christ.

> *"Neither is there salvation in any other: for there is none other name under heaven given among men, whereby we must be saved."*

In Philippians 2:9-11 we are also told:

> *"Wherefore God hath highly exalted him, and given him a name which is above every name: That at the name of Jesus every knee should bow, of things in heaven, and things in earth, and things under the earth; And that every tongue should confess that Jesus Christ is LORD, to the glory of God the Father."*

This is not only sound Christian doctrine, it is also the faith that God blessed when this nation was founded. Truly America has been blessed as no other nation because we have honored God's Son, Jesus Christ, like no other nation. Let us continue to bow before. . .

> *"The great God and our Savior Jesus Christ."*
>
> (Titus 2:13)

"Where The Spirit Of The LORD Is, There Is Liberty"

Ronald Reagan once said that:

> *"Freedom prospers when religion is vibrant and the rule of law under God is acknowledged. When our Founding Fathers passed the First Amendment, they sought to protect churches from government interference. They never intended to construct a wall of hostility between government and the concept of religious belief itself."*

On the contrary, the Bible itself explains that liberty is the bi-product of God's presence. In II Corinthians 3:17 we read: *"Where the Spirit of the LORD is, there is liberty."* However, if we as a people continue to offend the LORD and His laws, we will most certainly fall under His judgment. This is why we so desperately need a spiritual revival in our land today.

The Link Between National Humility
And National Renewal

This brings us to national humility. God did not bless America because we embraced liberty; we have liberty because we embraced God. If we ever get to thinking that we are blessed because we are better than others, we will have entered into the first stage of an arrogant national pride. Perhaps we are already there.

> *"God did not bless America because we embraced liberty, we have liberty because we embraced God."*

The second step in the wrong direction is when we put our trust in our military might as opposed to trusting in the LORD God. The Bible says:

> *"Woe unto them that go down to Egypt for help; and stay on horses, and trust in chariots, because they are many; and in horsemen, because they are very strong; but they look not unto the Holy One of Israel, neither seek the LORD!"*   (Isaiah 31:1)

Rather than trusting in our military might we must embrace the wisdom proclaimed by the Psalmist who declared:

> *"Some trust in chariots, and some in horses: but we will remember the name of the LORD our God. They are brought down and are fallen: but we are risen, and stand upright."*   (Psalm 20:7)

The difference of course is God! Yet when a nation is lifted up with a pride that disregards God, (step one) and then places its trust in military might, (step two) the third step naturally follows, which is to forget God and His laws. Thus, the Bible warns that:

> *"The wicked shall be turned into hell, and all the nations that forget God."*   (Psalm 9:17)

This same chapter in Psalms concludes with a prayer to remind us that we need God and His blessings. It says:

> *"Put them in fear, O LORD: that the nations may know themselves to be but men."*   (Psalm 9:20)

"If My People. . . Shall Humble Themselves"

All of this brings us back to II Chronicles 7:14, which not only speaks of prayer, but of national humility and repentance as well. We must remember that prayer without humility is an exercise in arrogance.

> **"Prayer without humility is an exercise in arrogance."**

National humility and repentance must precede national revival. When we look at our nation's history, in light of this truth, we find that we have always humbled ourselves before God. I have faith that deep down, America still recognizes our dependence upon God. I still have faith in America because America still has faith in God.

> **"I still have faith in America because America still has faith in God."**

Our job is to remind our people to honor God in our lives, our prayers, and in our public expressions of faith. Americans should attend and support the house of God on a regular basis. We should pray with our families at home. And, we should defend the faith once delivered to the saints, in every public forum. The very idea that some in Hollywood have the so-called *"constitutional right"* to blaspheme the name of our Lord and Savior, Jesus Christ, while wicked judges have the audacity to tell Christians that we cannot pray *"in Jesus name"* in our legislative assemblies is outrageous. We must not tolerate this intolerance!

Humility Gets Blessed.

In the Bible we see how God blessed both individuals and nations when they humbled themselves before Him. Even Nineveh, Israel's sworn enemy, found grace and averted certain judgment when both king and people humbled themselves before God, as a result of the preaching of Jonah. This is what the book of Jonah is all about. God wanted us to know that He is merciful to all people that honor Him. The Bible says:

"So the people of Nineveh believed God, and proclaimed a fast, and put on sackcloth, from the greatest of them even to the least of them. . . And God saw their works, that they turned from their evil way; and God repented of the evil, that he had said he would do unto them; and he did it not." (Jonah 3:5 & 10)

The principle of humility and repentance before God is applicable for nations as well as for individuals. Once again, the Bible says:

"God resisteth the proud, but giveth grace unto the humble. . . Humble yourselves in the sight of the LORD, and he shall lift you up." (James 4:6 & 10)

Chariots of Fire

Years ago, in the Academy Award winning film, *Chariots Of Fire*, this truth is vividly portrayed. In this true-life story, Scottish athlete, Eric Liddell, refused to run on Sunday, defying both king and country. As the race goes on without him, he is shown quoting verses from Isaiah chapter forty. We need to hear these words again today.

"Behold, the nations are as a drop of a bucket, and are counted as the small dust of the balance. Behold he taketh up the isles as a very little thing. . . All nations before him are as nothing; and they are counted to him as less than nothing, and vanity. . .He bringeth princes to nothing; he maketh the judges of the earth as vanity. . .

Hast thou not known? Hast thou not heard, that the everlasting God, the LORD, the creator of the ends of the earth, fainteth not, neither is weary? There is no searching of his understanding. He giveth power to the faint; and to them that have no might he increaseth strength. Even the youths shall faint and be weary, and the young men shall utterly fall; but they that wait upon the LORD shall renew their strength; they shall mount up with wings as eagles; they shall run and not be weary; and they shall walk and not faint." (Isaiah 40:15,17,23,28-31)

Again, Ronald Reagan got it right when he said:
> "*Freedom prospers only where the blessings of God*
> *are avidly sought and humbly accepted.*"

Humility is the key to obtaining heaven's blessings. We, as Americans, must once again humble ourselves before God.

"*Mark Them That Sigh And That Cry. . .*"

Ezekiel chapter nine records a very little known story, yet one that reveals the importance that God places on caring about one's country. At the time, Judea, and its capitol, Jerusalem, were in deep sin and apostasy. They had not only forgotten God, they actually spurned Him. Judgment was imminent. However, before God began pouring out his judgment upon Jerusalem, He sent an angel to perform a very important but peculiar task. In verse four below, God told the angel what to do:

> "*And the LORD said unto him, Go through the*
> *midst of the city, through the midst of Jerusalem, and*
> *set a mark upon the foreheads of the men that sigh*
> *and that cry for all the abominations that be done in*
> *the midst thereof.*"   (Ezekiel 9:4)

When judgment did fall, only those that had grieved over the sin of the city were spared! To me, this story illustrates the high premium that God places on those who care about their country. True humility involves grief and remorse for our own sins, as well as for the sins of our nation. Are we like those rare individuals in the story above? Only genuine concern will generate genuine prayer for our nation!

A Biblical Example of Revival Praying

Allow me to illustrate the importance of penitent revival praying, by looking at the prayer of Nehemiah. Remember it was under the leadership of Nehemiah that the city of Jerusalem was restored after the seventy years of captivity. This revival was important because it prepared Jerusalem for the coming of Christ. Listen to what happened and then consider Nehemiah's powerful prayer.

> "*And it came to pass, when I heard these words, that*
> *I sat down and wept, and mourned certain days, and*

fasted and prayed before the God of heaven, and said,
I beseech thee, O LORD God of heaven, the great
and terrible God, that keepeth covenant and mercy
for them that love him and his commandments: Let
thine ear now be attentive, and thine eyes open, that
thou mayest hear the prayer of thy servant, which I
pray before thee now, day and night, for the children
of Israel thy servants, and confess the sins of the
children of Israel, which we have sinned against thee:
both I and my father's house have sinned. We have
dealt very corruptly against thee, and have not kept
the commandments, nor the statutes, nor thy
judgments, which thou commandest thy servant Moses.
. . "   (Nehemiah 1:4-7)

Nehemiah then goes on to claim the promise of II Chronicles
7:14. As a result, God did indeed give Nehemiah His blessings, and
Nehemiah in turn encouraged others by saying:
"The God of heaven, he will prosper us; therefore
we His servants will arise and build." (Neh. 2:20)
God will do the same for us today!

"Except The LORD Build The House . . ."

In closing, allow me to quote King David who affirms the one
central truth of what this lesson is all about. He said:
"Except the LORD build the house, they labor in
vain that build it: except the LORD keep the city, the
watchman waketh but in vain. It is vain for you to rise
up early, to sit up late, to eat the bread of sorrows: for
so he giveth his beloved sleep. " (Psalm 127:1-2)

In spite of all the cares of his throne, King David could rest each
night, knowing that the LORD would not forsake him or his kingdom,
if Israel but trusted in Him. We also can take courage in this truth. If
American believers will forsake their sin and trust in the LORD, He
will not forsake us either. We have His word on it, for He clearly
promised, *"Blessed is the nation whose God is the LORD!"*
(Psalm 33:12)

Lesson Six: Open Book Quiz

(See how much you can remember. The answers are on page 245)

1. Which U.S. President said: *"Sometimes I can't help but feel the First Amendment is being turned on its head."?*_____

2. Complete the following statement by President Ronald Reagan: *"The _____ expression of prayer of our faith in God is a fundamental part of our _____ heritage and a privilege which should not be excluded from our _____ _____."*

3. Which U.S. President said: *"It is the duty of nations as well as men, to own their dependence upon the overruling power of God and to recognize the sublime truth announced in the Holy Scriptures and proven by all history, that those nations only are blessed whose God is the LORD."* ? _____

4. Which U. S. President said: *"We expect God to protect us in crises, but turn away from Him too often in our day-to-day living. I wonder if He isn't waiting for us to wake up."*? _____

5. Who said these words to the delegates of the Constitutional Convention: *"To that kind Providence we owe this happy opportunity... And have we now forgotten that powerful Friend? Or do we imagine that we no longer need His assistance?"*? _____

6. Which U.S. President said this about Christmas and democracy? *" 'Peace on earth, good will toward men' - democracy must cling to that message. For it is my deep conviction that democracy cannot live without that true religion which gives a nation a sense of justice and moral purpose."* ? _____

7. Which U.S. President said this about Christmas, as he lit the National Christmas Tree in 1950: *"At this time, we should renew our faith in God. We celebrate the hour in which God came to man. It is fitting that we should turn to Him. . . We can all pray. We should all pray."*? _____

8. Which U.S. President summed up the First Amendment with this statement: *"When our Founding Fathers passed the First Amendment, they sought to protect churches from government interference. They never intended to construct a wall of hostility between government and the concept of religious belief itself."*?

_____

The Liberty Tree
"All trees grow from the bottom up."

Lesson Seven
Spiritual Leadership & National Renewal

Dr. Lee Roberson once said: *"Everything rises and falls on leadership."* This is just as true in the spiritual realm as it is in the secular world. The greatest need in America today is for *spiritual* leadership. In this lesson I want to address the need for leadership at both the national *and* grass roots level. More importantly, I want to approach the need for spiritual leadership with *you* in mind. Everyone has a leadership role at some level. As you read this lesson, I ask you to see yourself as a spiritual leader in the battle for our nation's soul. It is also my prayer that you will catch the vision of what you can do to save your country as part of Prayer Force One.

Grassroots Leadership

Let me begin by addressing leadership at the grass roots level. Someone once said: *"Everything comes from the earth, even trains."* While I don't think the person who said this meant to leave God out, the quote does make its point. This is just another way of saying that *"All trees grow from the bottom up."* Even in politics, leadership at the grass roots level is recognized as irreplaceable. In this regard, there's an old campaign adage that states: *"All politics are local."* Even political leaders must have grass roots support, whether they are kings or presidents or prime ministers. As I quoted earlier, the Bible says:

> *"In the multitude of people is the king's honor: but in the want of people is the destruction of the prince."*

(Proverbs 14:28)

219

Movements too, even spiritual movements, must have grass roots support, and that means grass roots leadership. In almost every Biblical account, revival occurred only when the people themselves turned back to God. Even when God did raise up a national leader, it was usually in response to the prayerful cries of His people. (See the story of Moses and the various accounts recorded in the book of Judges, etc.)

When God made the promise of II Chronicles 7:14, notice that He says, "*If My people. . .* " Even God begins at the grass roots level. If America is to be saved, the participation of the people themselves is imperative. One man can plant an acorn but the tree must still grow from the bottom up.

National Leadership

While national revival cannot come without being embraced by the people themselves, this is not to take away from the role of leadership at the national level. Many times in the Bible we see how God sent a great revival because of the actions of a national leader such as Josiah, Hezekiah and Nehemiah.

At other times, great things happened only when a unique group of men came together to provide national leadership for the people. The birth of our own country bears testimony to this. The First and Second Continental Congresses and the Constitutional Convention itself, are three good examples of just how important united leadership can be. However, even these examples would not exist had it not been for the efforts of a much smaller group, which came to be known as the *Sons of Liberty*. Let me explain.

The Story Of The Sons of Liberty

Did you know that if it had not been for the efforts of a small band of tight-knit men from Boston, there might never have been a United States of America? History reveals that a small group of men including, such luminaries as Sam Adams, John Adams, James Otis, Dr. Joseph Warren, Paul Revere and others, formed an organization called the *Sons of Liberty*. Their example was then duplicated Across America until there were Sons of Liberty groups in almost every colony. The influence of the Sons of Liberty cannot be over-emphasized. Consider:

1. It was this *"Loyal Nine"*, (as they were originally called) who in 1765 organized a rally against the British Stamp Act, under what they called *"The Liberty Tree"*. In a speech on the floor of the British Parliament, Joseph Barre' referred to these men as the *"Sons of Liberty"*. Sam Adams and the Boston patriots were quick to adopt this name and embraced it as a term of honor.

2. It was the Sons of Liberty who organized the *Boston Tea Party,* one of the greatest *"public relations"* events in all of history.

3. It was Sam Adams and his Bostonian Sons of Liberty who organized the *Committees of Correspondence* throughout the colonies, which in turn, coordinated the many activities of the American independence movement.

4. It was Sam Adams and his Sons of Liberty who issued the call for the First Continental Congress of 1774. This is what really got things moving.

5. It was the Sons of Liberty who organized the *Committees of Safety* to stockpile weapons and gunpowder for the American resistance.

6. It was Paul Revere, William Prescott and William Dawes, all members of the Sons of Liberty, who rode to warn Lexington and Concord of the British approach. (Remember *"the shot heard 'round the world?"*)

7. It was Richard Henry Lee, a member of the Sons of Liberty, who made the resolution *"That these colonies should and of right ought to be free and independent states."* (Which resulted in the Declaration of Independence).

8. It was the Sons of Liberty who decided to promote a Southerner by the name of George Washington, as Commander of the Continental Armies, etc, etc.

I could continue to give many more examples but the thing to remember is that these men were local leaders who had a national impact. Without the leadership provided by Sam Adams, John Adams, James Otis, Paul Revere, Joseph Warren, William Prescott and others, the history of America and the world would be totally different.

God, Himself Is Looking For Spiritual Leaders

In Psalm 94:16 the LORD asks:

> *"Who will rise up for me against the evildoers? Or who will stand up for me against the workers of iniquity?"*   (Psalm 94:16)

You see, the problem is leadership. God is looking for someone to stand up against evil and point the way back home to Him. The LORD Himself plainly laments:

> *"I sought for <u>a man</u> among them, that should make up the hedge, and stand in the gap before me <u>for the land</u>, that I should not destroy it: but I found none."*
> (Ezekiel 22:30)

It comes down to this: national renewal, like anything else, relies upon leadership. This is why God is looking for brave and fearless leaders to minister to the nation. Again, the Bible states that:

> *"The eyes of the LORD run to and fro throughout the whole earth, to shew himself strong in the behalf of them whose heart is perfect toward him."*
> (II Chronicles 16:9)

According to this scripture, God is looking for people that He can bless in the struggle between good and evil. This nation is great because it was founded at a time when we had an incredible number of wise and godly leaders. God was able to work through these men, because they looked to Him, and followed His precepts. Today, we enjoy the benefits of their courage and labors almost two and a half centuries later. Look at what the Bible says concerning the legacy of such leaders.

> *"They that shall be of thee, shall build the old waste places: thou shalt raise up the foundations of many generations; and thou shalt be called, the repairer of the breach, the restorer of the paths to dwell in."*
> (Isaiah 58:12)

This is what America cries out for today. This is what God is looking for as well. In our land today, and at every level, we need a brave new generation of bold, moral leadership. This is what Prayer Force One is all about. We are asking *God* to raise up leaders of great courage and moral integrity, leaders with a spiritual dimension who also understand both the imperative and power of prayer.

"When The Righteous Are In Authority . . . "
In Proverbs 29:2 we read this statement:
> *"When the righteous are in authority, the people rejoice: but when the wicked beareth rule, the people mourn."*

In this scripture, I would like to draw your attention to four pairings of words. The first is the pairing of the words *"authority"* and *"rule."* We must realize that it does make a difference who exercises power. The second pairing are the words *"righteous"* and *"wicked,"* for our seats of leadership will be occupied by one or the other. The third pairing are the words *"rejoice"* and *"mourn,"* for we will either suffer or be blessed by the kind of people who hold office. The final pairing are the words *"people"* and *"people"*. Ultimately it is the people's welfare and happiness that are at stake in the nation. This is why we need to pray that God will give us godly rulers in our land and then to pray for our leaders as we are instructed to do in I Timothy 2:1-3.

Courageous Leadership In The Face Of Evil
Any people who protect immorality as a human right, sentence their own children to the ravages of sin. And any nation that will not defend the morality of its children from the vulgarity of the wicked, is destined to suffer destruction from within. Licentiousness must *never* be protected in the name of liberty. The immoral are shameless, and will not only take all the ground yielded to them, but will turn and rend the nation as their thanks. This is why George Washington deplored those who would undermine *"the twin pillars of religion and morality,"* which support the nation.

A nation does not have to bow to the will of the wicked. Evil and immorality can and must be opposed or it breeds like a cancer upon the whole face of the nation. The great English statesman, Edmond Burke put it this way.

> "*All that is necessary for the triumph of evil is for good men to do nothing.*"

Our own former President, Ronald Reagan, reversed the emphasis and said it like this:

> "*Evil is powerless when good men are unafraid!*"

Whichever way one states it, the path to national renewal must include courageous moral leadership at every level.

Gideon And His Three Hundred
(Found in Judges 6, 7 &8)

Beside the glorious example of our own nation's founding, there are numerous true stories from the Bible that serve to illustrate the truth of the point I'm trying to make. While most of these stories, being from the Old Testament, concern themselves with Israel, we must remember that:

> "*All these things happened unto them for ensamples: and <u>they are written for our admonition</u>, upon whom the ends of the world are come.*"
>
> (I Corinthians 10:11)

In Judges chapters 6-8, we find the story of Gideon. I love this story because when we are introduced to Gideon, we find a timid and skeptical young man. The Bible says that God sent an angel, who said to Gideon, "*The LORD is with thee thou mighty man of valor!*"

Now, you have to understand that just one verse before, we are told that Gideon was hiding wheat for fear of the Midianites. I think maybe Gideon looked around to see whom the angel was talking to, for he certainly knew that he himself was no mighty man of valor.

When Gideon came to his senses, he also revealed his skepticism as he protested saying: "*If the LORD be with us, where be all the miracles that our fathers told us of?*" The thing I think the LORD seeks to teach us in this story is that He can use people who don't really look that good on paper. On at least three occasions in the story we find that Gideon remains fearful as he moves forward in obedience. The truth is that God is simply looking for men and women who are great enough to be little enough to be used. He is looking for people that move forward by faith in spite of fear and obstacles. This is what real courage is all about.

In order to further develop Gideon's faith, God then required him to reduce his army from 32,000 to just 300 men! By this we are to understand that:

"There is no restraint to the LORD to save by many or by few." (I Samuel 14:6)

Our confidence must rest solely on the promises of the LORD, and not on the arm of man, for. . .

"The weapons of our warfare are not carnal, but mighty through God to the pulling down of strong holds." (II Corinthians 10:4)

Gideon obtained a great victory by God's hand through a combination of obedience, faith, and a God-given plan. Gideon instructed each man to get a pitcher containing a little oil lamp and a trumpet. Gideon's last words of instruction were these: *"When I come to the outside of the camp, it shall be that, as I do, so shall ye do."* Then, at the given moment, Gideon broke his pitcher, revealing the flame within, as he cried out, *"The sword of the LORD and of Gideon."* Then Gideon began blowing his trumpet with all his might. Upon seeing his example, each of his three hundred soldiers followed suit, doing the same thing. You can imagine the *"shock and awe"* which the enemy felt as they fled in disarray.

I encourage you to read all three chapters in the book of Judges. As you do, please take note at what an ordinary man can do when he is obedient to the LORD. God can send a national deliverance against impossible odds and through unlikely people, if they just take courage and follow the LORD. Perhaps you are the very person God is looking for. Perhaps you are another Gideon, or another of Gideon's three hundred.

Leadership And Nationhood

God ordained the establishment of three institutions: the family, the church and the nation. Today we find that all three of these God_ordained institutions are under attack. We are well aware that the sanctity of marriage and the Biblically defined home are under attack. Many are becoming aware that the church too, is under siege, with *"thought police"* fining the church for so called political involvement. Imagine, a society where everyone is free except the one institution whose sole purpose is to do good! How ridiculously absurd!

However, what many Americans are unaware of is that the concept of nationhood is also under attack. Even before the facts to support this reality are laid before them, American workers instinctively sense that they are being sold out to some globalist agenda that is not in our national interest. They are beginning to realize that while the state is growing stronger and stronger, the nation itself is growing weaker and weaker. Here again, leadership, or should I say, the lack thereof, is at fault.

> *"While the state is growing stronger and stronger, the nation itself is growing weaker and weaker."*

"Art Thou He Who Weakened The Nations?"

In the book of Isaiah, we find a curious statement concerning Satan. In Isaiah 14:9 we have a prophecy that refers to the time when Lucifer will be cast into the common hell. The event is described in detail as we read:

> *"Hell from beneath is moved for thee to meet thee at thy coming: it stirreth up the dead for thee, even all the chief ones of the earth; it hath raised up from their thrones all the kings of <u>the nations</u>."*

Now before we continue, be sure and get the context of the passage. Here we have the devil being cast into hell before the kings of the nations. Pay particular attention to the word *"nations"*, for we see it again as the inhabitants of hell respond to his arrival:

> *" All they shall speak and say unto thee, Art thou also become weak as we? Art thou become like unto us? Thy pomp is brought down to the grave... How art thou fallen O Lucifer, son of the morning! How art thou cut down to the ground, <u>which didst weaken the nations</u>!"* (Isaiah 14:10-12)

While I am tempted to quote the rest of this amazing prophecy, the thing that I want to point out is that it is the work of the devil to weaken the nations. (For only weakened nations, like weakened homes, are susceptible to his wiles.) <u>Never forget that it is the work of Satan to weaken nations</u>! This is a very important Biblical principle.

Who's Minding The Store?

With the above truth in mind, Americans must wake up and realize that our nation is growing weak because many of our leaders are preoccupied with globalization at the expense of our national sovereignty. It is becoming clear that these internationalist global objectives are taking precedence over our own genuine national concerns.

When I went to college in the seventies, I worked at Inland Steel, the largest single-site producer of steel in the world. Today, Inland Steel is gone, and its great American rival, U.S. Steel, is barely producing what it produced back in 1902! I also worked at Pullman Standard, one of the greatest railcar producers in history. Today, the great Pullman Car Company has been liquidated. In my own home town of Oklahoma City, General Motors just shut down, and Dayton Tire is also moving out. This trend can be found nationwide! Why? Because our leaders have forgotten that nationhood matters.

> *"Our leaders have forgotten that nationhood matters!"*

Today, nations are being turned into international trade zones while ownership of American companies and American interests are being moved out of the country or sold to foreign investors who have no loyalties to America or the American worker. The plain simple truth is that no one is minding the national store!

> *"The plain simple truth is that no one is minding the national store."*

Foreign Domination Is A Judgment Of God

In the Bible, every time Israel turned her back on God, He allowed them to be occupied by a foreign power. Foreign dominance and oppression was almost always the means that God used to punish Israel for dishonoring God and His laws. These six occupations are recorded in the book of judges.

- To the Mesopotamians for eight years, Judges 3:8
- To the Moabites for eighteen years, Judges 3:12-14
- To the Canaanites for twenty years, Judges 4:2-3
- To the Midianites for seven years, Judges 6:1
- To the Ammonites for eighteen years, Judges 10:7-8
- To the Philistines for forty years, Judges 13:1

The seventh time they turned their back on God, occupation gave way to seventy years of foreign captivity, and finally to a total dispersion among the nations. (Their return is setting the stage for the end time events prophesied in the Bible.)

America's Wealth And Jobs Are Being Exported

In like manner, the United States is now seeing the ever growing encroachment of foreign powers. We, as a nation, are losing out on two fronts. In one direction, American wealth and American jobs are being exported with wholesale abandon. American companies are being *"internationalized"* as the accumulated wealth of four centuries is being invested overseas. In the other direction, foreign powers have acquired majority ownership of our U.S. national debt. (A dangerous reality) Remember, the Bible says that: *"The borrower is servant to the lender!"* (Proverbs 22:7)

In February of 2006, ABC reported that foreign entities now own more than 53% of the U.S. federal debt in publicly traded world markets. To further complicate this dangerous imbalance, consider also that Communist China has reached a trillion dollars in international reserves, 70% of which are in held in dollar notes and bonds. David Bloom, Director of Strategy of HSBC Global Markets, (One of the world's largest banking service groups with over 9,500 offices in 76 countries.) was recently quoted as saying *"The U.S. needs a trillion dollars a year just to stand still."* Columnist Dana Smith recently asked, *"What happens when China sells off all those dollars and trades them for Euros? You guessed it, a financial nightmare."*

Economist Bob Chapman of *The International Forecaster*, recently predicted that,*" In the severe recession we are entering now,* (certain politicians) *will argue that we have to form a North American Union to compete with the Euro."* Perhaps this will be the excuse that globalist politicians will use to engulf America into the new world order. If such a scenario does indeed happen, it will mean the end of America as we know it!

To further complicate the threat, American companies are creating a huge sucking sound as they export real American jobs overseas. Giants such as Microsoft, Citigroup, Hewlett-Packard, Proctor & Gamble, AT&T and AIG have all exported their call centers to foreign countries. According to Forrester Research, U.S. companies are expected to send over 3.3 million jobs overseas in the next twelve years. CNN is even maintaining a list of the companies that are going overseas in a report called *"Exporting America." (Read it on the web.)*

America Must Lead The World, Not Be Overcome By It!

I do not believe that God is through with America. The United States must not only survive in a global world, it must also continue to lead it! However we must never allow our country to lose what our fathers died to preserve: *freedom* and *independence*. This old world still needs *"One Nation Under God."* This is what makes us different. This is what gives hope to the rest of the world. In spite of the outgoing tide, I for one believe America can still be saved. However, it is going to take leaders at every level who understand the spiritual dimension required to do battle for our nation. In short, I believe that God is still looking for spiritual leaders for today.

I believe that each of us can and must do our part to aid our country in this hour. We can no longer afford the luxury of complacency. There are those in powerful places who would integrate us into some global society in which we would cease to be rulers of our own destiny. We must not abdicate our responsibility and allow others to choose our national course for us. It's our country too, and here, the people rule!

I am asking each of you to do what you can as a leader within your respective field of influence, to preserve a free and Christian America. More than ever before, we must remember that : *"Now is the time for all good men to come to the aid of their country!"*

The Challenge Before Us

I began this book with a story about Ronald Reagan. I think it also fitting to close with a quote from his now famous 1964, *Rendezvous With Destiny* speech. Listen carefully to his words:

> *"Alexander Hamilton warned us that a nation which prefers disgrace to danger is prepared for a master and deserves one. . . If we are to believe that nothing is worth the dying, when did this begin? Should Moses have told the children of Israel to live in slavery rather than dare the wilderness? Should Christ have refused the Cross? Should the patriots at Concord Bridge refused to fire the shot heard round the world? Are we to believe that all the martyrs of history died in vain?*
>
> *You and I have a rendezvous with destiny. We can preserve for our children this, the last great hope of man on earth, or we can sentence them to take the first step into a thousand years of darkness. If we fail, at least let our children, and our children's children say of us, we justified our brief moment here. We did all that could be done."*

In doing all that we can do, let us never forget that the greatest thing that we can do is to pray. Prayer is still *"force one!"* I am asking each of you to make humble prayer, *"force one"* in your personal life; to make it *"force one"* in your family's life; and to make prayer, *"force one"* in your nation's life too. Together, and with God's help, we can make a difference!

Lesson Seven: Open Book Quiz
(See how much you can remember. The answers are on page 245)
1. Complete this statement by Dr. Lee Roberson: "*Everything rises and falls on* _____."
2. Fill in the blanks in this quote from Proverbs 14:28. "*In the multitude of* _____ *is the king's honor: but in the want of* _____ *is the destruction of the prince.*"
3. What was the name of the small group of men that helped to bring about the American Revolution? _____
4. Fill in the blanks in this quote from Psalm 94:16: "*Who will rise up for me against the* _____? *Or who will stand up for me against the workers of* _____?"
5. According to Isaiah 58:12, godly leaders would:" Raise *up the* _____ *of many generations.*"
6. List the four pairings of words in Proverbs 29:2.

_____ & _____
_____ & _____
_____ & _____
_____ & _____

7. Complete this statement by Edmond Burke: "*All that is necessary for the triumph of evil is for good men to do* _____."
8. Complete this statement by President Ronald Reagan: "*Evil is powerless when good men are* _____!"
9. Fill in the blanks in this scripture from I Samuel 14:6. "*There is no restraint to the LORD to save by* _____ *or by* _____."
10. Fill in the blanks in this scripture from II Corinthians 10:4. "*The* _____ *of our warfare are not carnal, but* _____ *through* _____ *to the pulling down of strong holds.*"
11. According to Isaiah 14:12, one of the works of Satan is to _____ *the* _____.
12. Compete this well-known statement. "*Now is the time for all good men to come to the aid of their* _____!"
13. Complete this quote by President Ronald Reagan. *We can* _____ *for our children this, the* _____ *great hope of man on earth, or we can sentence them to take the first step into a thousand years of* _____."

Every day, I pray over America, and dream of a time when a great move of God will sweep across our land. Please join me in this prayer. Perhaps *you* could start a Prayer Wing too.

Appendix A
How To Start A Prayer Force One
Prayer Wing
In Your Home, Church Or Workplace

The secret to prayer is praying. We can talk all day about prayer but until we get on our knees and pray, it does no good. God said, *"Call unto me, and I will answer thee, and shew thee great and mighty things, which thou knowest not."* (Jeremiah 33:3) However, the burden of sending our prayers heavenward is totally upon us. By the same token, we can talk all day about building a prayer movement in obedience to God's command, but until we actually become a part and do it, we will accomplish little. Let me ask you three questions.

1. Did you pray for America today?

2. Did you pray for America yesterday?

3. Did you pray for America the day before yesterday?

Whether you answered yes or no, you're just what we're looking for. If you said yes to these questions, you have demonstrated that you are sincerely burdened for America. Why not recruit others to pray with you as part of a Prayer Force One *Prayer Wing*?

If you answered no to any of the above questions, there is room for improvement. Why not make the commitment today to mend your ways and become a prayer warrior for America?

"Every Great Movement Of God Begins In Prayer"
In his autobiography, Pat Robertson tells of how God taught him early on, the importance of prayer and the power of the Holy Spirit through a story about the early ministry of Billy Graham. It seems

that Billy Graham's 1949 Los Angeles crusade had come to a crossroads of ending or moving into the realm of the miraculous. Most of us know the story of how William Randolph Hearst put Billy on the *"front page"* of his papers. What most of us don't know is how God used a little lady by the name of Mrs. Edwards to encourage prayer for Billy Graham. It seems that this Mrs. Edwards, a lady of about sixty to seventy years of age, had decided to travel at her own expense to promote prayer for the ministry of Billy Graham.

One night, Billy Graham announced that he would have to make a decision of whether to continue or close the Los Angeles crusade. Mrs. Edwards called her prayer group to meet for an all night prayer meeting. They not only prayed that the meeting would continue, but that God would pour out His Spirit upon Los Angeles in revival. As they prayed, they sensed a powerful presence descend upon the room. Some were frightened, and all were conscious of this presence. They discussed the phenomenon and then agreed that since they were asking for God's blessings and fullness of the Holy Ghost, that the presence must be of the LORD. (Luke 11:11-13)

As the ladies continued in prayer, the phone rang. It was Billy Graham, who cried out, *"Are you ladies praying for me again? I'm here in my hotel room so filled with the Holy Spirit I can't sleep. I've been pacing the floor and preaching to the walls and furniture. I can't stop."*

That night the ladies knew that God had answered their prayers. The Los Angeles meeting did continue as revival descended upon the city. This meeting soon became the national sensation that catapulted Billy Graham and his small band of helpers into six decades of evangelistic success. The testimony of this story also changed Pat Roberson's life and ministry.

This story clearly illustrates what America needs again today. If we are to have revival in America, we must have the hand of God touch us and the power of the Holy Spirit anoint our efforts. To this end we are encouraging prayer groups to form all across America for the single purpose of praying for a heaven-sent, spiritual revival in our land. Perhaps God would use you to help such a prayer group to form in your home, church or workplace. I offer the following suggestions on how to best go about doing this.

Suggestions On How To Start and Conduct
A Prayer Force One *Prayer Wing*

1. The first and most important suggestion is to start your *Pray Wing* on purpose and with a purpose. From the very outset, define what your purpose and goals are.

2. If you are starting this as a ministry *in* your local church, be sure and obtain the blessings of your pastor or proper church authorities.

3. Decide on a regular once a month meeting time and stick with it so that people will come to expect the meeting. Suggested times might be before or after a regular evening church service, or on an off-night during the week.

4. Write or e-mail *Prayer Force One* to tell us of your *Prayer Wing*. Send the names and addresses (including the e-mail addresses) of the leaders and participants in your group. In this way, we will be able to send e-letters and special bulletins about our efforts and special prayer events.

5. Before your first meeting send out a proper invitation to all that might be interested in coming. Encourage each of these to invite other friends to the meeting. Use the telephone to call and remind those interested. Do this the day before the planned meeting.

6. Encourage attendees to bring a small dessert or finger food for a fellowship to follow.

7. Try to follow a planned schedule. This will help the meeting to flow and prevent abuse of the participants' time. There should be a starting time and an ending time. I suggest a schedule something like this:

> **A.** Start with an opening prayer at the appointed time.
> **B.** The host should introduce the purpose of the *Prayer Wing* and have each attendee introduce themselves.
> **C.** At the first meeting, elect a *Prayer Wing Captain* and *Co-Captain*. Ideally, this should be from among those who have taken the initiative to start the *Prayer Wing* in the first place. These people must be dedicated to seeing that the *Prayer Wing* stays active, planning each meeting and coordinating with national entities.

D. Use the book, *Prayer Force One: Across America*, during the first seven meetings. Ask the participants to acquire their own copy. Use the seven lessons in Part II during the first seven meetings. You will also find helps from our web site to aid your monthly meetings.

E. Have a time of prayer. If the group is small, you can use the round-robin approach, giving each an opportunity to pray. Or, if the group is larger, you can divide men and women, or even into pairs to pray.

F. After the prayer time, break for refreshments and fellowship. Be sure and end at the appointed time so that attendees will want to come back.

I feel that I should also add a few words of caution. Be careful not to allow the *Prayer Wing* to become a political forum. We neither endorse candidates nor political parties. However, we do stand for Bible-based family values, and need to stay abreast on things to pray about that may affect the Christian foundations of our nation. (See our *Statement of Faith & Values* posted on our web site.) See also page 59 for requirements for using the *Prayer Force One* name and logo. Although your *Prayer Wing* is an independent prayer group, we must still maintain the integrity of the *Prayer Force One* name.

Also be careful that no one is allowed to *"take over"* or take advantage of the meeting for some ulterior motive. It is important to stay on-point and keep our purpose and goals in mind.

Finally, let me encourage your *Prayer Wing* to coordinate your efforts with those of Prayer Force One's national effort. You, as a *Wing Leader or Co-Wing Leader,* will, from time to time, receive exclusive memorandums from *Prayer Force One.* By cooperating and working together, we truly become a spiritual force of one! May God bless you and your own local *Prayer Wing* as we work together to save our nation.

Appendix B
How To Become A Christian
A Serious Discussion About Biblical Salvation

Dear Reader, let me ask you the most important question that you will ever face. All eternity will depend upon your answer. *Are you saved?*

"Saved?" You say. *"What is that?"*

Well, saved is a very important Bible word. It is used many, many times in the Word of God. In fact, in just this one short but serious chapter, I will show you sixteen different passages from the Bible which use this very important word. If you will stay with me, by the time we get done, you will know what being saved means and whether or not you are saved. Most importantly, I will show you *from the Bible* how to be saved!

So Simple That A Child Can Understand

To begin, let's listen to what Jesus said in the Gospel of Matthew. *"And Jesus called a little child unto him, and set him in the midst of them, and said, Except ye be converted, and become as little children, ye shall not enter into the kingdom of heaven."* (Matthew 18:2-3)

And again, in Mark 10:14 Jesus said, *"Suffer the little children to come unto me and forbid them not: for of such is the kingdom of God. Verily, I say unto you, whosoever shall not receive the kingdom of God as a little child, he shall not enter therein."*

You see, the concept of being saved is so simple that a child can understand it. Even a little child can know whether they are saved or not. Unfortunately, many adults do not know if they are saved. My prayer for you, the reader, is that you will read this chapter to the end, and then, as a little child, receive this soul saving Bible message and be saved.

Saved From What?

"Well," you may say, *"Saved? Saved from what?"* And, you would be right in asking such a question, for the very idea of being saved implies a certain *'lostness'* or impending peril. It suggests that we are in the grip of something that can harm or even destroy us. All of these definitions of being saved are actually taught in the Bible.

Lost In Sin!

In II Corinthians 4:3-4 the Apostle Paul wrote, *"But if our gospel be hid, it is hid to them that are <u>lost</u>: In whom the God of this world hath blinded the minds of them which believe not, lest the light of the glorious gospel of Christ, who is the image of God, should shine unto them."*

You see, the Bible teaches that we are lost and in dire need of a Savior because of our sin. Sin is the breaking of God's law. It is comprised of the multitude of our selfish and wicked acts which we have committed against God. The Bible is very clear about this, and we are <u>all</u> guilty. In Isaiah 53:6 we read: *"<u>All</u> we like sheep have gone astray; we have turned every one to his own way; and the LORD hath laid on him the iniquity of us <u>all</u>."*

<u>All</u> means everyone; you, me, and every person who has ever lived. The Bible again indicts <u>all</u> when it says: *"For <u>all</u> have sinned, and come short of the glory of God."* (Romans 3:23) And again we read: *"There is <u>none</u> righteous, no, not one."* (Romans 3:10)

Oh friend, it is so necessary for each one of us to own up to the fact that we have sinned against God. We have <u>all</u> sinned against our holy Creator. Because of our sins, we are under condemnation and in need of being <u>saved</u>.

We are also told what the punishment for our sin will be when the Bible says: *"For the wages of sin is death!"* (Romans 6:23) This death is twofold. It is first a physical death, However, the Bible also teaches us that this will include a second or spiritual death as well. The Bible says: *"And as it is appointed unto men <u>once</u> to die, <u>but after</u> this the judgment: so Christ was once offered to bear the sins of many; and unto them that look for him shall he appear the second time without sin unto salvation."* (Hebrews 9:27-28)

Saved From The Wrath of God

This *"after death judgement"* is referred to in the Bible as *"the second death"* or *"hell"*. We read about this in Revelation 21:8. It says: *"But the fearful, and unbelieving, and the abominable, and murderers, and whoremongers, and sorcerers, and idolaters, and all liars, shall have their part in the lake which burneth with fire and brimstone: which is <u>the second death</u>."* This is what the Bible means when it says: *"Being now justified by his blood, we shall be <u>saved from wrath</u> through him."* (Romans 5:9)

Oh thank God that Jesus came to <u>save</u> us from the wrath to come! Dear reader, Jesus will either be your judge or your Savior. It all depends on what you do with His gospel message. This difference can be clearly seen when the Bible says: *"And to you who are troubled rest with us, when the Lord Jesus shall be revealed from heaven with his mighty angels, in flaming fire taking vengeance on them that know not God, and that obey not the gospel of our Lord Jesus Christ: Who shall be punished with everlasting destruction from the presence of the Lord, and from the glory of his power; When he shall come to be glorified in his saints, and to be admired in all them that believe (because our testimony among you was believed) in that day."* (II Thessalonians 1:7-10)

Go back and re-read this passage of scripture. Do you not see yourself as one or the other. You cannot be both. Jesus Christ will either be your Savior or judge. He died on Calvary's cross so that you might be <u>saved</u> from the wrath to come. Do you not now begin to see that being <u>saved</u> is the most important thing to get settled in your entire life?

We Cannot Save Ourselves!

Perhaps, you agree with the Holy Scriptures that we have been discussing. Perhaps God's sweet Spirit is already pricking your heart with His saving love. Perhaps you are saying, *"I must do something in response to what the Bible says."*

This is all good. But, we must also recognize that there is <u>nothing</u> we can do to <u>save</u> ourselves. Just as a pauper cannot pay his own debts, so we are helpless to pay for our sins. We have no righteousness with which to atone for our sins. Our only recourse is to throw ourselves upon the mercy of God and the salvation that only Jesus can bestow.

This is what the Bible means when it plainly explains *why* God <u>saves</u> people. In Titus 3:5 we read, *"Not <u>by works</u> of righteousness which we have done, but according to his mercy he <u>saved</u> us."*

We see this again in II Timothy 1:9-10 when Paul tells why God saves us. He wrote: *"Who hath <u>saved</u> us, and called us with an holy calling, <u>not according to our works</u>, but according to his own purpose and grace, which was given us in Christ Jesus before the world began, but is now made manifest by the appearing of our Savior, Jesus Christ, who hath abolished death, and hath brought life and immortality to light through the gospel."*

This is again made abundantly clear in the book of Ephesians, where we read: *"For by grace are ye <u>saved</u> through faith; and that not of yourselves: it is the gift of God: <u>not of works</u> lest any man should boast."* (Ephesians 2:8-9)

In all of these passages of scripture, we see some variation of the words *"<u>not of works</u>"*. This is because, as lost sinners, we can do nothing to <u>save</u> ourselves. We are already ruined. We have nothing to give in exchange for our soul. This is why we need, *"<u>A Savior!</u>"*

Jesus Christ Came To Save Sinners.

We now come to the greatest truth in all the Bible. We have arrived at the very heart of the gospel message. Jesus came to <u>save</u> us! Jesus came to <u>save</u> you! This is the sum and substance of the good news of the gospel. Time and again, Jesus himself told us why he came. Jesus said: *"For the Son of man is come to seek and <u>to save</u> that which is lost."* (Luke 19:10)

Jesus also said: *"For the Son of man is not come to destroy men's lives, but <u>to save</u> them."* (Luke 9:56) In the verse that comes after the familiar and world famous John 3:16, we read: *"For God sent not his Son into the world to condemn the world; but that the world through him might be <u>saved</u>."* (John 3:17)

In fact, every word of Jesus was spoken for the purpose of saving souls.

Notice what He said in John 5:34: *"But these things I say, that ye might be saved!"*

When the archangel, Gabriel, gave instruction to Joseph concerning the birth of Jesus through the virgin Mary, he said: *"And she shall bring forth a son, and thou shalt call his name JESUS: for he shall save his people from their sins."* (Matthew 1:21)

Perhaps the great Apostle Paul summed it up best for all of us when he said, *"This is a faithful saying, and worthy of all acceptation, that Christ Jesus came into the world to save sinners; of whom I am chief."* (I Timothy 1:15)

Your Lost Soul Is Important To God.

Dear one, time and time again Jesus expressed the importance of your lost soul. Jesus said: *"For what shall it profit a man, if he shall gain the whole world, and lose his own soul? Or what shall a man give in exchange for his soul?"* (Mark 8:36-37)

Likewise, in the fifteenth chapter of Luke's gospel, Jesus told several stories, each illustrating the importance of our soul to God. In the first story, Jesus tells how the good shepherd left the ninety-and-nine to go and find one lost sheep. When the shepherd found it, Jesus said: *"Rejoice with me, for I have found my sheep which was lost. I say unto you, that likewise joy shall be in heaven over one sinner that repenteth, more than ninety and nine just persons, that need no repentance."* (Luke 15:6-7)

My friend, your soul, like the helpless lost sheep, is important to: *"God our Saviour; who will have all men to be saved, and to come unto the knowledge of the truth."* (I Timothy 2:3-4) This is why Jesus said: *"I am the good shepherd: the good shepherd giveth his life for the sheep."*

In the next story, the story of the prodigal son, we see our souls, which, though wasted in riotous living, are very dear to the Father. Jesus tells us what happened when the broken and disgraced prodigal returned home. In Luke 15:20-24 we read: *"And he arose and came to his father. But when he was yet a great way off, his father saw him and had compassion, and ran, and fell on his neck, and kissed him. And the son said unto him, Father, I have sinned against heaven, and in thy sight, and am no more worthy to be called thy son. But the father said unto his servants, Bring forth the best robe, and put it on him; and put a ring on his hand, and shoes on his feet: And bring hither the fatted calf, and kill it, and let us eat and be merry: For this my son was dead, and is alive again; he was lost, and is found."*

Friend, your soul is very dear to the Heavenly Father, and he has provided for your salvation. But, the cost was also very dear!

Salvation Cost God His Son!

The cost of your salvation was the sacrifice of Jesus Christ. In what is probably the best known verse in all the Bible, John 3:16, we find: *"For God so loved the world, that he gave his only begotten Son, that whosoever believeth in him should not perish, but have everlasting life."*

Oh no, salvation was not cheap! The redemption of man was purchased by the blood of Jesus Christ, for nothing else would do. In I Peter 1:18 we read: *"Forasmuch as ye know that ye were not redeemed with corruptible things, as silver and gold, from your vain conversation, but with the precious blood of Christ, as of a lamb without blemish and without spot."*

During the last supper, Jesus gave the cup to the disciples which pictured his own shed blood. In Luke 22:20, Jesus said: *"This cup is the new testament in my blood, which is shed for you."*

In Colossians 1:14 the Bible speaks of God's dear Son and then says: *"In whom we have redemption, through his blood, even the forgiveness of sins."* And later in verse twenty, the same chapter says that God, *"Made peace through the blood of his cross!"*

Rejecting Christ Leaves Us Condemned.

You see dear reader, the cross of Jesus Christ and His shed blood is the only way to God and forgiveness. The Bible is adamant about this! In Acts 4:12, Peter preached this boldly when he said: *"Neither is there salvation in any other: for there is none other name under heaven given among men, whereby we must be saved!"*

The Bible gives many unmistakable and very clear warnings about rejecting Christ. In Hebrews 10:29 it says: *"Of how much sorer punishment, suppose ye, shall he be thought worthy, who hath trodden under foot the Son of God, and hath counted the blood of the covenant, wherewith he was sanctified, an unholy thing, and hath done despite unto the Spirit of grace?"*

It is a very serious thing to reject the offer of salvation. In fact, the Bible makes clear, that in view of the salvation freely offered by God, rejecting Christ is ultimately the reason that men remain condemned. In John 3:18 we read: *"He that believeth on him is not condemned: but he that believeth not is condemned already, because he hath not believed in the name of the only begotten Son of God."*

The Man In The Middle

Perhaps you remember seeing a painting depicting the crucifixion of Jesus Christ. You will no doubt recall that two thieves were crucified with Christ. The eternal destiny of each of these men was determined by what they did with the man in the middle.

Of the first thief, we read these words: *"And one of the malefactors which were hanged railed on him, saying, If thou be Christ, save thyself and us." (Luke 23:49)*

This man mocked Jesus, using the word "if", indicating unbelief. Do you know what Jesus said to him? . . . Not a single word! This is because God never responds to unbelief! To obtain salvation, we must embrace the truth of the gospel, based on God's word, by faith! Hebrews 11:6 teaches us: *"But without faith it is impossible to please Him; for he that cometh to God must believe that He is, and that He is the rewarder of them that diligently seek him."*

Today Thou Shalt Be With Me In Paradise!

Now look how different the encounter was between the second thief and Christ. In Luke 23:40 we continue the narrative: *"But the other answering, rebuked him saying, Dost not thou fear God seeing thou art in the same condemnation? And we indeed justly; for we receive the due reward of our deeds: but this man hath done nothing amiss. And he said unto Jesus, <u>Lord</u>, remember me when thou comest into thy kingdom."*

You see, the second man believed and called upon Jesus, saying Lord! Oh how differently Jesus responded to the second sinner! Notice what Jesus said: *"And Jesus said unto him, Verily I say unto thee, today shalt thou be with me in paradise!" (verse 43)*

How To Be Saved

This brings us to one of the most prominent promises in all of the Bible. In Romans 10:13 we read: "For *whosoever shall call upon the name of the Lord shall be <u>saved</u>."*

Just as the man on the cross called upon the name of the Lord, so may any man, woman, boy or girl today. Salvation is just that simple! Jesus did the hard part. Jesus did the dying. So too, Jesus will do the saving! The only thing we have to do is to repent of our sins, and call on Christ to <u>save</u> us. He will do the rest. For: *"The word is nigh thee, even in thy mouth, and in thy heart: that is the word of faith which we preach; That if thou shalt confess with thy mouth the Lord Jesus, and believe in thine heart that God hath raised him from the dead, thou shalt be <u>saved</u>!"* (Romans 10:8-9)

You see, salvation is just a prayer away. All you have to do is to call upon Christ Jesus to <u>save</u> you, for he promised: *"For whosoever shall call upon the name of the Lord shall be <u>saved</u>!"* (Romans 10:13)

Do it now, this very minute. The Lord is listening, and will do as he has promised. Pray a simple and sincere prayer of faith something like this: *"Dear Lord, I am a sinner, and I need the Savior. I believe that Jesus Christ is Your Son and that He died on the cross and shed His blood for me. I believe that You raised Him from the dead. Lord, please come into my heart and life and <u>save</u> my soul. I ask this in Jesus name, Amen."*

Oh friend, do it now! After you have sincerely prayed to receive Christ as Savior, sign your name and the date, so that you will always remember the day you were <u>saved</u>! When you are finished, write or e-mail us and let us know of your decision.

On this day_____, I prayed and asked Jesus Christ to be my Lord and Savior. I believe that Jesus died for my sins, and that he rose again from the dead. I am trusting His finished work on the cross to save my soul.

(Signed:)

Appendix C
Answers To Quizzes

Lesson One:

1. So help me God.
2. A prayer; John Adams
3. The Bible
4. All of them
5. The laws of God
6. Self government; Christianity
7. Bible; rock
8. duty; nations
9. the LORD
10. Woodrow Wilson
11. hope; faith; Bible
12. God; Supreme Being
13. Ronald Reagan
14. George H. W. Bush

Lesson Two:

1. duty; Christian; Christians
2. Patrick Henry
3. George Mason
4. Benjamin Franklin
5. John Witherspoon
6. Religion; education; religion; God
7. religion; liberty
8. *New England Primer*
9. Noah Webster

Lesson Three:

1. A tornado or hurricane
2. Fort McHenry
3. Francis Scott Key
4. *The Star Spangled Banner*
5. 1931
6. 1864; Lincoln
7. religious faith; spiritual; resource
8. Twenty-three
9. His grace
10. Our fathers' God
11. President Ronald Reagan; Sir Winston Churchill; Robert Kennedy; President Richard M. Nixon
12. prayer
13. affirm; God

Lesson Four:

1. sacred; covenants
2. stones; memorial
3. landmarks; fathers
4. The U. S. Supreme Court
5. The U. S. Supreme Court
6. The U. S. Supreme Court
7. Franklin Roosevelt
8. George Washington
9. under God
10. Laus Deo; Praise be to God
11. Ronald Reagan; George H. W. Bush
12. George W. Bush
13. In God We Trust

Lesson Five:

1. Leviticus 25:10
2. a nation; people
3. forget God
4. Abraham Lincoln

5. spiritual; evil; public
6. a Christian nation
7. 20,000
8. Christian; Christian; Christianity
9. war; cradle
10. one
11. Dwight D. Eisenhower

Lesson Six:

1. Ronald Reagan
2. Public; American; public schools
3. Abraham Lincoln
4. Ronald Reagan
5. Benjamin Franklin
6. Franklin D. Roosevelt
7. Harry S. Truman
8. Ronald Reagan

Lesson Seven:

1. leadership
2. people; people
3. The Sons of Liberty
4. evildoers; iniquity
5. foundations
6. authority; rule
   righteous; wicked
   rejoice; mourn
   people; people
7. nothing
8. unafraid
9. many; few
10. weapons; mighty; God
11. weaken; nations
12. country
13. preserve; last; darkness

BIBLIOGRAPHY

Adams, John Quincy. Lives of Madison and Monroe. Philidelphia: J. L. Gihon, 1854

Barton, David. The Myth Of Separation. Aledo, TX: Wallbuilder Press, 1992

Cassell, Clark. President Reagan's Quotes. Washington, DC: Braddock Publications, 1984

DiCianni, Ron. The Faith Of The Presidents. Lake Mary, FL: Charisma House, 2004

Federer, William J. America's God And Country: Encyclopedia of Quotations. Coppell, TX: Fame Publishing, 1994

Graham, Billy. Just As I Am. New York: HarperCollins, 1997

Harnsberger, Caroline Thomas. Treasury Of Presidential Quotations. Chicago: Follet Publishing Company, 1964

Irving, Washington. The Life Of Washington, New York/London: Co-operative Publication Society, Nd

Johnson, William J. George Washington The Christian. Milford, MI: Mott Media, 1976

Johnson, William J. Abraham Lincoln The Christian. Milford, MI: Mott Media, 1976

Kengor, Paul. God And Ronald Reagan. New York: HarperCollins, 2004

McCollister, John God And The Oval Office. Nashville: W Publishing Group, 2005

McCullough, David. Truman. New York: Simon & Schuster, 1992

Peabody, Salem H. American Patriotism. New York: John B. Alden, 1886

Reagan, Michael. The Words Of Ronald Reagan. Nashville: Thomas Nelson, 2004

Reagan, Ronald. Where's The Rest Of Me? New York: Duell, Sloan & Pierce, 1965

Reagan, Ronald. In His Own Words. New York: Touchstone, 2001

Order Form

Help spread the message of Prayer Force One!

(Use the order form on the back of this page.)

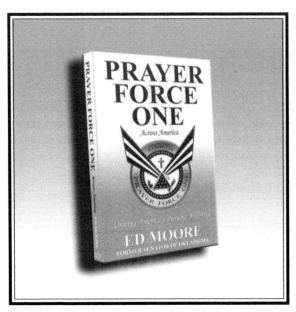

Prayer Force One: Across America is available in any quantity from one book, to a case(s). (36 books per case) Prices are listed below.

1 copy - $11.99
2-4 copies - 10% discount (@$9.99 each)
5 - 199 copies - 40% discount (@7.19 each)
200 - 499 copies - 50% discount (@ 5.99 each)
500 or more - 40% discount less 25% (@5.39 each)
For large orders, please order by the case. (36 books to a case)

Christchurch Publications
P. O. Box 270
Newalla, OK 74857

Telephone orders : (405)-386-3226
Web sites: <www.ChristchurchPublications.com> or,
<www.PrayerForceOne.com> Thank you for your order.

Quick Order Form
Prayer Force One: Across America

Number of copies:_____(x) $11.99 = Preliminary total $_____
(Line 1)

Enter discount amount: $_____
(Line 2)

> To figure your discount amount, multiply total on line one times your discount percentage. (See previous page.) *Example:* If you ordered 10 copies, you would multiply the cost of ten books [$119.90] x [.40]. This is your discount amount. Enter it above on line two.

Enter your *subtotal* by subtracting line two from line one. $_____
(Line 3)

Enter your *shipping* total on this line. (see chart below) $_____
(Line 4)

Enter your *grand total* by adding lines 3 and 4. $_____
(Line 5)

Total Amount Enclosed: $_____

INFORMATION:

Name:_____Phone_____

Shipping Address_____

City_____ ST_____ Zip_____

E-mail Address _____

Shipping Charges

1 book	$1.79
2-4 books	$1.00 for each book
10-35 books	$0.50 for each book
Per case (36 books)	$12.61 per case
Bulk Order	FOB (Call for amount)

Christchurch Publications • P.O. Box 270 • Newalla, OK 74857